CHOICE   MAY '73
Performing Arts
Music

WILLIAMS, Peter. Figured bass accompaniment. Edinburgh (dist. by Aldine), 1971 (c1970). 2v 69-16012. 17.50.   ISBN 0-85224-054-6

Students and teachers alike will benefit from a study of these volumes. The text of volume I offers a brief history of the art of continuo playing, including organ continuo. Changing styles of accompaniment are presented. The earliest basso-continuo style, Italian, German, English, and French basso styles all receive detailed treatment. Realizations from 1600-1800, and the most important types of accompaniment are covered. Instruction is given in executing every theoretical and technical problem one might encounter in realizing a figured bass, i.e., trills, slides, acciaccaturas. Volume II deals with the "grammar" of figured bass. "Advice to Players" is given before each exercise. This volume is an anthology of graded examples for the soloist and keyboard player taken from "real" music. Examples include Corelli, Bach, Purcell, to name a few. Three fully worked realizations are presented. The "Handlist of Books" and "References" are excellent. An indispensable work, essential to the study of accompaniment, figured bass, and harpsichord playing, which should be in the hands of all music majors.

281

see AM 64: 91-117. July-Dec 1992
"The Règle de l'Octave in thorough-bass
theory & Practice" by thomas Christensen.

on how to harmonise contiguous notes in any octave

Aria Quarta.

Ere seluaggie, Che per môti errate Il piè fermate In queste verdi

piaggie V dit'il mio lamento ch'a ta lor per pietà ferma to il ven to.

Illide mia Mia filli de bella M'è si rubella si spietat',e ria Che mi

vede morire Che mi vede mo rire ne vuol moré d'il mio cordo glio v

di re.

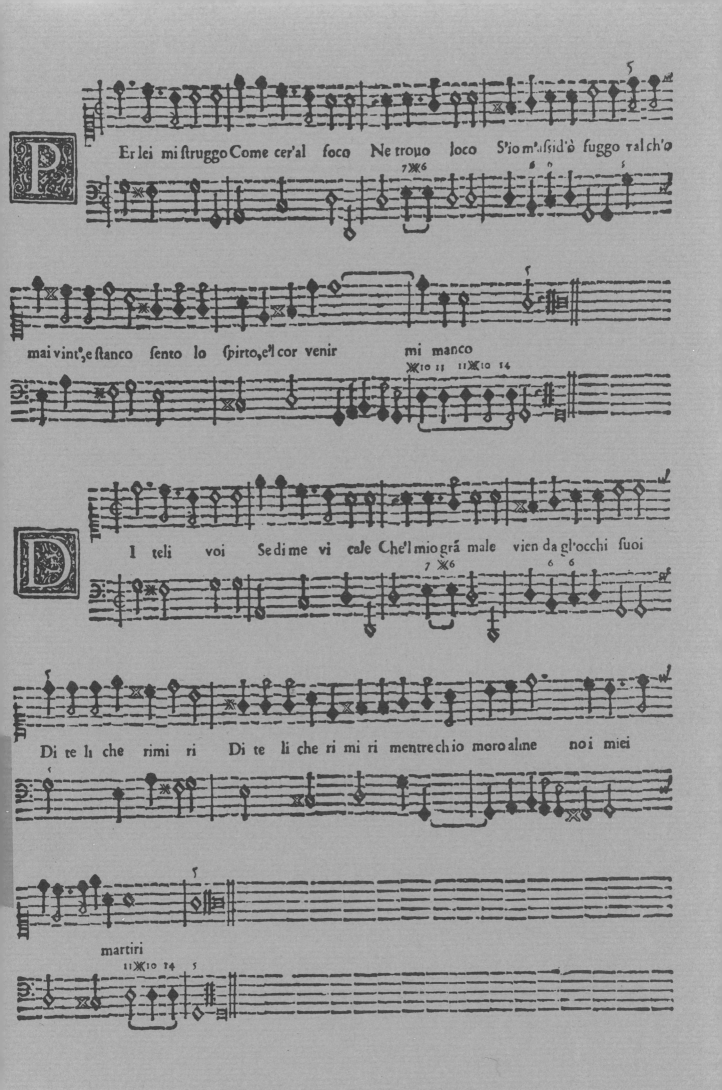

VOLUME ONE

FIGURED BASS ACCOMPANIMENT

... and if my book is not enough to support you in your
studies and to meet all your wishes, you may be
certain that having learned so much, *Usus te plura
docebit*–practice will teach you more.

F. Gasparini *L'Armonico pratico* 1708

1

FIGURED
BASS
Accompaniment

PETER WILLIAMS

AT THE

UNIVERSITY PRESS

EDINBURGH

© Peter Williams, 1970

EDINBURGH UNIVERSITY PRESS

22 George Square, Edinburgh

ISBN 0 85224 054 6

North America
Aldine Publishing Company
529 South Wabash Avenue, Chicago

Library of Congress
Catalog Card Number 69-16012

Printed in Great Britain by
Spottiswoode, Ballantyne and Company Ltd

The end-papers show the song 'Fere selvaggie'
from Giulio Caccini's *Le Nuove Musiche*, 1602,
pages 31 and 32. See Volume 2, page 101, for a
transcription with additional figuring.

PREFACE

From the author's point of view, the most important sentence in this work is to be found in the introduction:

'Several important assumptions govern the form of this book, it being possible to describe the fine art of *continuo*-playing in as many ways as there are players.'

I am conscious that this is only one way to cover a subject whose immensity has not only discouraged any comprehensive account previously but has caused the form of this particular account to change radically in the course of its writing. It began as an anthology of realizations from the period 1600–1800 followed by a series of exercises for players today; it became enlarged to include salient points from all the composers' and theorists' advice known to me, and hence to include a brief history of the whole art of *continuo*-playing. In its final form the book owes much to Mr Walter Cairns of Edinburgh University Press, whose help went far beyond that normally given by publisher's editor.

For assistance in securing material, I am grateful to many librarians, notably Mr Michael Anderson (Edinburgh), Dr Luisa Cervelli (Rome), S. Vinicio Gai (Florence) and Dr Oskar Mischiati (Bologna). It was the playing of my teachers Thurston Dart and Gustav Leonhardt that aroused my interest in the art of Figured Bass, and the special opportunities given by the Russell Collection of Harpsichords and Clavichords in the Department of Early Keyboard Instruments (University of Edinburgh) that encouraged the writing of the book.

Peter Williams

Unsigned painting of an instrumental consort, sixteenth century (Bourges, Musée du Berry). The stylized grouping is paralleled in a further painting by the same artist, showing four unaccompanied singers performing from manuscript part-books. The four instruments are pentagonal spinet, lute, recorder and probably violone. It was the kind of group found during two centuries of secular music-making and containing instruments for different functions: (*a*) a treble melody, (*b*) varied harmonic accompaniment, (*c*) a firm bass line. There is no question here of lute, spinet and violone playing from a figured bass part, and the painting shows that there was nothing essentially new in what became known as *basso continuo* groups.

CONTENTS

INTRODUCTION

The first requirement of a *continuo*-player is that he play correct chords. But although some players quickly learn to do this for at least the simpler figures, none will play *continuo* well without historical knowledge, practical experience, and harmonic sensitivity, or without understanding his instrument and his rôle in the music concerned. This book attempts to deal with theory, practice, and history in the belief that they are or should be inseparable. In general, Volume One is to be read, Volume Two to be played; but there are practical examples to be played in Volume One, as there is theoretical advice to be read in Volume Two, and both practice and theory are necessary for any player wishing to learn even the first things about the art of figured-bass accompaniment.

The playing of even simple chords from figures is sufficiently difficult to remain beyond the grasp of many musicians. Yet because the technique was of immense importance to two centuries of music, no musician can afford to be without some idea of its purpose and effect in written music. As a study, *continuo*-playing embraces both the musical and the musicological. It is therefore with both these aspects in view that I have listed the contemporary advice in Chapter 2 and the historical styles in Chapter 3. Some things the player can learn from books: how to play the figures, what keyboard style was most likely in the composer's mind as he wrote the piece to be played. But others he cannot: how to support the soloist, how to direct a small ensemble, what precisely to play while the soloist rests. It is tempting to advise, as J.S.Bach and others did, that the student learn by word of mouth from the experienced player, that he learn the art beyond mere figures by watching and imitating the 'best masters'. But this is now dangerous advice, for today's 'best masters' have largely invented a manner of their own that has little to do with the intentions or, equally important, the expectations of any figured-bass composer. When well done this manner is charming and even, sometimes, powerful; but it can also be so easily out of style that the music inevitably loses some of its original characteristics. Many of the players who are anxious to solicit the audience's attention have great technical skill, but the good *accompanist* must never divert attention from the soloist's part, even if occasionally he can best do this by imitating it or vying with it.

Several important assumptions govern the form of this book, it being possible to describe the fine art of *continuo*-playing in as many ways as there are players:

(i) The player's first requirement is to know the chords. To do this he must recognize the figures, be proficient at the keyboard, and have a sense of harmony that will sustain him when the figures are inadequate—as they are almost bound to be. Because all the chords can be illustrated by very short examples, little space in the book is devoted to the figures themselves. Chapter 1 is a brief list of the chords to appear in the figured-bass period; *it should be taken slowly and carefully*, the player not moving on until he has perfected the examples of each chord given in Volume Two. There is no short cut. Players will find it an advantage to cultivate the automatic reaction: to be able to play at sight such chords as $\begin{smallmatrix} 4 \\ 2 \end{smallmatrix}$ $\begin{smallmatrix} 4 \\ 3 \end{smallmatrix}$ $\begin{smallmatrix} 5 \\ 2 \end{smallmatrix}$ and $\begin{smallmatrix} 7 \\ 4 \\ 2 \end{smallmatrix}$ on any note of the keyboard is invaluable, and a few dull exercises to encourage this ability do no harm.

(ii) Chapter 1 will not be the player's sole source of information on classical harmony. Almost every figured-bass player will be familiar with the nature of diatonic harmony in some form, most probably as written exercises for examinations. No writer of figured-bass tutors in the seventeenth and eighteenth centuries could assume so much, nor does even the most astute of them describe his harmonic language in the simple terms that time-perspective enables us to do. On the other hand, misleading though this theory of Inversions may be for a true or theoretical understanding of diatonic harmony, it remains the best means of explaining figured basses to the player.

(iii) All players, especially the least experienced, will learn figured-bass accompaniment best when they are playing 'real' music. They may even find themselves understanding the figures more quickly if they are able to think less about chords and more about serving the soloist's melody. There is no reason why from the earliest moment they should not learn to accompany an actual or imaginary soloist. Although in the light of later experience a player may see that the art in accompanying Schütz's easy recitative is more elusive than he once thought, he can nevertheless accompany much of this and other composers' music as soon as he has learnt to play root-position triads in the simplest keys. On the other hand, even the best composers—J. S. Bach, Handel, Mozart, Beethoven—at times taught or were themselves taught by means of figured-bass exercises as dull and divorced from real music as those of any Victorian textbook. A few exercises are therefore included in Volume Two, but the least dull have been chosen. Throughout the anthology, the examples are taken from the period of figured bass: from theory-books and from 'real' music.

(iv) The most useful, important and enlightening *continuo* instrument is the harpsichord. Although the art of organ *continuo* occupies an important proportion of this and any figured-bass study, the harpsichord is the instrument implied throughout the greater part of this book, as indeed it was the instrument implied by most composers of the period. For the purpose of learning figured bass, of course, perfect harmonic sense of every example can be made on the piano. But students should regard the piano as only a substitute for the harpsichord, since quite apart from *timbre* the piano will not produce the textures of true *continuo*-playing. Authors of Quantz's generation who praised it had a delicate type of fortepiano in mind, and modern pianos are irrelevant for players wishing to learn the finer points.

(v) Although the player's enjoyment tends to increase as the music makes stylistic demands on him, he will make every effort to match technical skill with historical knowledge. Chapter 2 lists some of the problems that will arise for a conscientious accompanist. The background knowledge, to which this chapter is an introduction, is as difficult to acquire as technical skill, for it is easy to be way-laid by pedantry, irrelevance or vanity. It is indeed difficult to say which of these does most harm. Although many players seem chiefly activated by vanity, it is well to remember that this is so often expected of them; many a conductor requires the harpsichord-player to act as quasi-soloist, as if instrument and player were hired only to be conspicuous. But if he is fully aware of the nature of his instrument, of the idioms employed by accompanists in the period concerned, and of the style and demands of the piece before him, the *continuo*-player should be able to resist the temptation to add 'extemporized' frills. The harmony should always be his first concern.

(vi) The art of accompaniment differed from period to period, area to area, *genre* to *genre*, and there is no such thing as a universally 'correct' way to play figured-bass *continuo*. But there is very often a correct way to play a specific piece of figured-bass *continuo*. Chapter 3 accordingly describes the most important types of accompaniment in terms of theoretical sources and written-out realizations of the period. Some of these realizations are more important than others; a few are obviously exceptional and were written down because they were not typical. On the whole, however, I think that written-out realizations are more trustworthy as examples of current practice than may appear to the casual reader.

(vii) 'Taste' is not a vague, unattainable gift but something which can be acquired by combining wide knowledge with experience. Lutenists in Monteverdi's operas, harpsichordists in Purcell's songs, organists in Bach's Passions, pianists in Mozart's early concertos—all these players extemporized *continuo* parts which were decorative in some degree at certain points in the work. The problems are: where are these points and what should be played at them? There is overwhelming evidence that accompanists played more adventurously whenever the soloist rested between phrases or during the introduction to an aria; Chapters 2 and 3 suggest what they may have played on these occasions. One might go so far as to say that the room for opinion and for personal taste, which so often means wayward improvization, is very small.

In Volume Two, the suggestions for *continuo* realization have been incorporated into the examples rather than discussed in the text. In learning the art of figured-bass accompaniment there is no substitute for experience; no amount of theorizing, no sets of 'rules' (which never existed), no lists of hints for the accompanist (which are forbiddingly difficult to formulate) can replace the experience which comes through performance with others. The player should copy or reject my suggestions as his taste or knowledge directs: but he should first examine them to see whether they are designed to support the composer's own music (the solo and bass lines), whether they are in the correct musical style, and whether they avoid the temptation to write the composer's music for him. For convenience, almost all of the examples are for soloist and keyboard-player alone, with no other instrument except a cello; this is not a sign that in orchestral or choral works the *continuo*-player can allow himself greater licence. On the whole he should allow himself less, his energy being directed towards making his harmonies and rhythms heard—the harmonies doubled, the rhythms reiterated, the texture enriched.

Further details of the theory-books referred to throughout Volumes One and Two will be found in the Handlist of Books on page 107 of Volume One.

1

THE CHORDS

TRIADS

1.   The root-position triad is the simplest of the chords and is rarely given figures in a *basso continuo* part. However, one of the following might occur when the bass is ambiguous:

3	5	8	8	8		8
			3	5		5
						3

All of these, whether one figure or three, show that the notes to be added above the bass are the 3rd, 5th and 8ve. In the scale of C major the root-position chords are as follows:

Example 1

to avoid emphasising the diminished 5th B-F

For the convenience of the right hand or for variety of texture, the notes above the bass can be differently distributed:

Example 2

etc.

2.   If the music is very difficult, the bass-line moving quickly, or the player confused, play the bass only, without chords. Bass lines and steady beats are both far more important than the chords.

If circumstances are less dire, try parallel 3rds or 10ths. These are especially convenient above a quick-moving bass, but do not overuse them. Extra parts might be added on the beat:

Example 3 C. P. E. Bach

A single figure 3 can denote a row of parallel 3rds:

Example 4 Albrechtsberger

C. P. E. Bach points out that parallel 3rds are not easy in a minor key if augmented intervals between adjacent notes are avoided – as they should be.

3.   Accidentals are necessary for some chords in the minor scale, or when the piece modulates from its original key:

$$\sharp 3 \quad \flat 3 \quad \natural 3 \quad \sharp 5 \quad \flat 5 \quad \natural 5$$
$$3\sharp \quad 3\flat \quad \text{etc.}$$

Accidentals are often used by themselves as a short-hand device:

$$\sharp \quad \flat \quad \natural \; = \; \sharp 3 \quad \flat 3 \quad \natural 3$$

4.   5ths are perfect in major triads and are rarely figured. But sometimes $\sharp 5$, 5 and $\overset{\shortmid}{5}$ are used to indicate that the 5th is perfect or augmented, depending on context. Thus the B major chord in Example 5 may appear in the figures as

$$\sharp 5 \text{ or } \overset{\shortmid}{5} \text{ or } \sharp 3 \text{ or simply } \sharp$$
$$\sharp \qquad \sharp$$

since major 3rds imply perfect 5ths.

Example 5

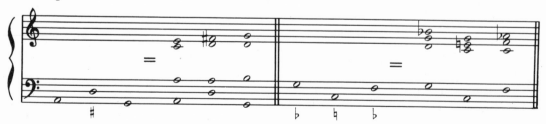

Some composers write the flattened 5th (♭5) as $\not{5}$, but this can usually be distinguished from $\natural5$.

5.   When playing any chords, avoid obvious consecutive 5ths and 8ves by changing the position of the right-hand chord:

Example 6

not

and playing in contrary motion.

Consecutives in outer parts should be avoided, but in inner parts they are often tolerable. If the harmony is full – more than four parts – or the other instruments and singers are numerous, consecutives are generally of no importance.

6.   A line ——— below a note or group of notes indicates that the previous chord is held (or restruck) against a moving left-hand bass line:

Example 7

is played

More often than not, however, the line was omitted.

7.   For chords of the First Inversion, the full figuring is $^8_6{}_3$, but 8 is usually omitted, as is 3 unless it requires an accidental. Even then, the accidental may replace the figure.

Example 8

8.   For chords of the Second Inversion, the full figuring is $^8_6{}_4$, but $^6_4$ is the usual abbreviation. Accidentals may be added to either figure.

Example 9

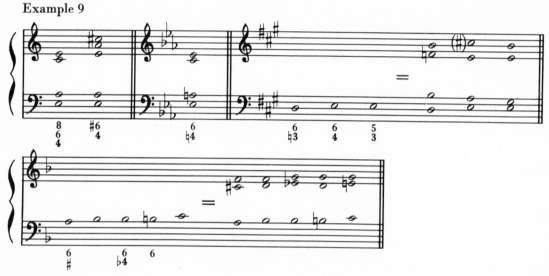

9.   The sign $\bar{6}$ is the most common way to write $_{\#3}^6$ or even $_{\flat3}^6$:

Example 10

10.   In Example 11, to avoid consecutives (a), the major 3rd will sometimes need to be doubled. The two 3rds sound well at the top and bottom of the chord (b) but may result in a spacing too wide to suit the tone of the harpsichord; (c) would therefore be best. The leading note should not be doubled (d) as both would need to rise to the tonic:

Example 11

11.   In slow music, consecutives can be easily avoided (a); but to avoid them in lively-to-fast music, it may be best to omit the fourth part and play the $^6_3$ chords with only three notes (b). Three parts are especially convenient for parallel $^6_3$ chords.

In a minor key, the augmented 2nds in such progressions as (c) are best avoided ; but, as C. P. E. Bach noted, sometimes they can contribute to the mood of the piece (d):

Example 12

DOMINANT AND OTHER SEVENTHS

1.   All chords of the 7th are discords or 'incomplete sounds' that require resolution to other chords, usually concords. 'Discord' does not mean harsh dissonance; the piquant effect of a discord can be, in the words of J. C. Heck, 'far more agreeable' than concords.

2.   Irrespective of the number of parts, the full figuring of the 7th is $^7_5\!:_3$

Example 13

7 alone is the most common indication with or without an accidental ($\sharp 7$, $\flat 7$). Some composers wrote $\not{7}$ for $\flat 7$.

10

3.   In resolving, the 7th (the 'discordant' note) falls, whether the rest of the chord does or not (*a*). Parallel 7ths 'not by oversight but set with design' (C. Simpson) are also commonly met with (*b*):

Example 14

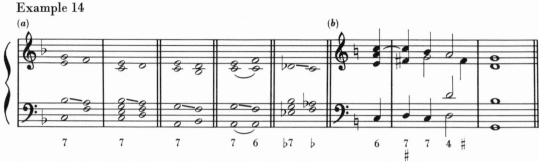

4.   Each of the figures in a 7th chord can have an accidental before it, depending on key and context. Accidentals can utterly change the nature of the chord:

Example 15

5.   The figure for the First Inversion of dominant and other 7ths is $\frac{6}{5}$ or, more commonly, $\frac{6}{5}$. In many works, ♭5 or $\cancel{5}$ alone indicates this chord.

Example 16

However, ♭5 or $\cancel{5}$ ought strictly to indicate a simple diminished triad, without the 6th (no B in the last part of Example 16).

6.   The figures for the Second Inversion of dominant and other 7ths are $\frac{6}{4}$, or, if the 6th needs no accidental, $\frac{4}{3}$:

Example 17

7.   The figures for the Last Inversion of dominant and other 7ths are $\overset{6}{\underset{2}{4}}$, or, if

the 6th needs no accidental, $\overset{4}{\underset{2}{}}$. 4+, indicating the sharpened 4th, is a common abbre-

viation for the $\overset{6}{\underset{2}{\sharp 4}}$, a vital chord in Italian recitative :

Example 18

A quick way of interpreting a $\overset{6}{\underset{2}{4}}$ chord is to play a triad on the note above the bass.

THE DIMINISHED SEVENTH

1.   The so-called diminished 7th chord can be written as a flat-seventh chord:

$\flat 7$ $\overset{\flat 7}{\flat 5}$ $\overset{\flat 7}{3}$ $\overset{\flat 7}{\underset{3}{5}}$ etc., depending on context :

Example 19

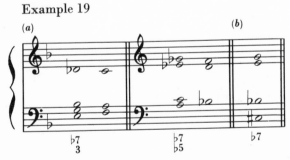

The $\flat 7$ is the usual figuring when the bass note is either a leading-note to the following chord (a), or a note already or newly sharpened (b).

    J.S.Bach's* rule-of-thumb was 'with $\flat 7$ where there is also a $\sharp$ in front of the
bass note, one plays the 3rd and 5th'.

---

*In this chapter, 'J.S.Bach' refers to the composer's additions of 1738 to Niedt's *Musicalische
Handleitung* (see Handlist, page 108). The musical examples marked 'Handel' are taken from
recitatives in the Italian cantatas for solo voice.

12

2.   However, the 'diminished 7th' chord can be written as a sixth chord, de-
depending on the context:  etc.

Example 20

3.   The ♭7 figuring often indicates that the note resolves downwards, the $\frac{6}{4}$
figuring that it resolves upwards; but the player should trust his ear more than
his eye. Composers are not good orthographers.

Example 21   **Handel**

4.   Enharmonic changes can also obscure the progressions:

Example 22   Rameau, *Code*

Note that ♯2 or ♮ alone can (and usually does) indicate the complete diminished
7th chord.

5.   If the chord was obvious, composers often did not figure it:

Example 23 Handel

Moreover, any *appoggiature* introduced by the singer do not affect the figuring.

6.   Despite the apparent complexity of diminished 7th figuring, pianists will know that in an equally tempered scale there are basically only three diminished 7th chords, all the others being inversions of those three.

Learn to recognize the figures as simple formulae rather than as complex chords. The diminished 7th is a very easy chord.

7.   Full diminished 7ths are not always necessary. In such a recitative as the following, distinguish between the diminished 7th (*a*) and the simpler $^{\#6}_{\natural3}$ (*b*) by omitting the 5th in the latter chord:

Example 24 Handel

SUSPENSIONS

1.   The three suspensions popular in the period of figured bass were 4–3, 7–6 and 9–8. Basically they all consist of (*a*) concord, (*b*) discord, (*c*) concord:

Example 25

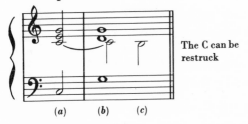

The C can be
restruck

As in this example, the 4–3 suspension normally contains a 5th in both chords:

5   5
4   3

14

2.   The 7–6 suspension has the 3rd in both chords, but rarely the 5th: $\begin{smallmatrix}7&6\\3&3\end{smallmatrix}$

Example 26

3.   For the 9–8, a fuller chord (with four different notes) can usually enrich the suspensions; 'with 9–8 one plays the 3rd and 5th', as J. S. Bach wrote.

Example 27

The 9–8 suspension frequently occurs at cadences in the *galant* period (*b*).

4.   As discords, the notes suspended should be 'prepared'–on the organ by holding the note over from the previous chord:

Example 28 J. F. Daube   F. Geminiani

OTHER DISCORDS

1.   Several of the 'other discords' have already been met in the section on Dominant and Other Sevenths. For example, the $\begin{smallmatrix}4\\2\end{smallmatrix}$ is often identical with the $\begin{smallmatrix}6\\4\\2\end{smallmatrix}$, an inversion of a dominant or secondary 7th chord. Since, however, every player of the figured-bass period to some extent learnt his harmony by means of unexplained *formulae*–the extent varied from country to country, period to period– modern accompanists should also learn the chords as certain sounds on the keyboard. To be able to play immediately a $\begin{smallmatrix}5\\2\end{smallmatrix}$ chord above *any note of the scale*, with-

out needing to consider that it is probably a 'suspension in the bass resolving on to a First Inversion triad', is infinitely more useful than being able to 'explain' it and its harmonic context.

2.   The $\frac{4}{2}$ may occur by itself with no further figure, especially in Italian music. In many cases, however, the figuring $\overset{6}{\underset{2}{4}}$ is intended:

Example 29

'With $\frac{4}{2}$ one plays the 6th', according to J. S. Bach; but if in doubt, play a simple $\frac{4}{2}$. Similarly, the figure 2 alone indicates a $\frac{4}{2}$, usually a $\overset{6}{\underset{2}{4}}$ while the crossed $\cancel{2}$ very likely indicates a diminished 7th chord, as already shown:

Example 30

3.   The $\overset{5}{\underset{2}{4}}$ usually denotes a suspension in the bass, the resolution being a 7th chord in First Inversion:

Example 31

4.   The $\overset{6}{\underset{2}{4}}$ may denote a bass suspension, the resolution being a 7th chord in root position. The $\overset{6}{\underset{2}{\sharp4}}$ may be abbreviated to $\sharp4$. A further version $\overset{6}{\underset{\sharp2}{4}}$, which was common in eighteenth-century Germany, may appear as $\sharp2$ or $\cancel{2}$:

Example 32

5.   The $\frac{4}{2}$ can descend to the note whose triad is anticipated by the figures (a), or it can be a triple *appoggiatura* suspension (b):

Example 33

The second resolution is very familiar in Italian recitative throughout the period.

6.   The figure $\frac{5}{2}$ may also occur by itself. In the work of most composers of the period, $\frac{4}{2}$ and $\frac{5}{2}$ appear more often than the three-figure chords $\frac{6}{4}{}_2$ and $\frac{7}{5}{}_2$.

As with all 'thin' chords, the discordant note of the $\frac{5}{2}$ is best played in close position for richness of effect:

Example 34

7.   The $\frac{6}{5}{}_2$ chord appears as an *appoggiatura*, often chromatic in the music of 1750 or so:

Example 35 C. G. Schröter

8.   The $\frac{7}{5}$ usually resolves on to a First Inversion triad; or it may, like all other discords, ignore the resolution and pass to another chord:

Example 36   Rameau *Traité*

9.   The $\frac{\sharp7}{6}4$ is usually a chord of the diminished 7th above a pedal point; so is the $\frac{7}{5}\sharp3$, as in the following examples:

Example 37 Handel   Couperin *Règle*

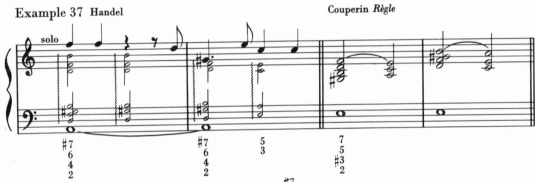

The figuring for the first chord is usually $\frac{\sharp7}{4}2$.

10.   The $\frac{7}{5}4$ or, written another way, $\frac{9}{7}5$, is a compound *appoggiatura*, belonging chiefly to the later eighteenth century:

Example 38

It may occur in earlier recitative in place of the conventional $\frac{7}{4}2$, but J. S. Bach told his students that 'with the $\frac{7}{4}2$ nothing else is played'.

THE NATURE OF DISCORDS IN FIGURED BASS

1.　　To take one chord as an example: the $\begin{smallmatrix}7\\4\\2\end{smallmatrix}$

Example 39

may be a $\begin{smallmatrix}5\\3\end{smallmatrix}$ triad in C major whose bass is delayed by (*a*) suspension, (*b*) *appoggiatura*, or (*c*) accented passing-note:

Example 40

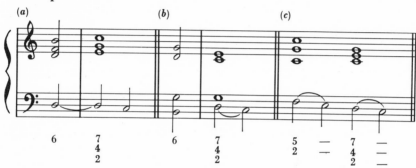

On the whole, however, *appoggiature* and suspensions are more often found in the upper parts than in the bass.

2.　　Such chords may resolve differently—with (*a*) the inner parts rising as *appoggiature*, (*b*) the three upper parts rising, and (*c*) all four parts moving by step:

Example 41

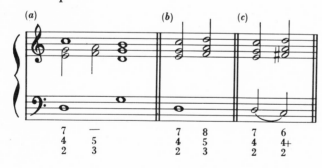

3.　　Most seventeenth- and eighteenth-century harmony was simple enough for players to require a few conventional formulae, but by 1730 Rameau observed that they were inadequate for the new harmonic possibilities. Nevertheless, even in the more complex sections of J.S. Bach's cantatas, such a figure as $\begin{smallmatrix}7\\4\\2\end{smallmatrix}$ would almost certainly indicate one of the three resolutions in Example 40. In Italian recitative, the $\frac{7}{4}$ was nearly always a compound *appoggiatura* – with or without the 5 or 6, it resolves on to the 'tonic':

Example 42 Handel

See also Example 37.

4.   Similarly, the $\frac{5}{4}$ chord was nearly always followed by a $\frac{5}{3}$ on the same bass, although both may be highly decorated:

Example 43

Exceptions were dramatic, especially in recitatives:

Example 44

But even here, the C rightly falls to the B.

5.   In much music of about 1580–1680, especially in Italy, it was understood that a suspension decorated the cadence, without the composer troubling to write it in or to figure it. Even the most knowledgeable of modern scholars often forget this when they make new editions of such music.

Example 45 Monteverdi *Orfeo*, Act v

written

played

According to A. Scarlatti, some players also added the dominant 7th to the resolution, whether figured or not; but to some tastes this weakens the cadence.

6.   Throughout the period 1600–50, the $\frac{5}{4}$ was the most common discord, forming the harmonic climax of many phrases, especially when the resolution anticipated the subsequent chord and was therefore itself dissonant.

Example 46 Schütz *Saul*

voices

Saul,   Saul,   Saul, Saul,   was ver-folgst du   mich?

organ
bass

Gasparini (1708) and others recommended holding the 4th over against its resolution on the harpsichord, producing a fairly severe clash–

Example 47 A. Scarlatti

which inspired, or was inspired by, 4 + 3 dissonances in other instrumental music:

Example 48 H. J. F. Biber, Sonata v, 1681

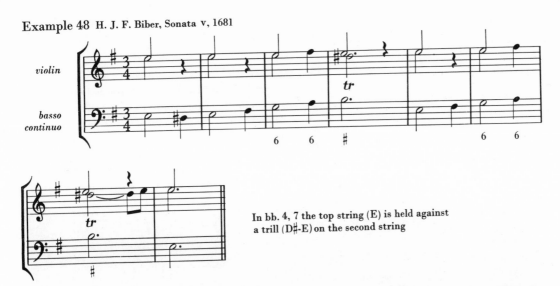

In bb. 4, 7 the top string (E) is held against
a trill (D♯-E) on the second string

Penna (1672) had previously suggested similar harmonies for the organ. This is a type of *acciaccatura*, one of the keyboard-player's idiomatic devices treated in the next chapter.

Title page of Agostino Agazzari's *Del Sonare sopra'l Basso con tutti li strumenti e dell'uso loro nel concerto* (Siena 1607), one of the earliest accounts of figured bass, its origins, its realization and its scoring. The instruments pictured include both those 'of foundation', which sustained the general harmony (keyboard and, when light accompaniment is needed, plucked string instruments) and 'of ornamentation', which 'make the harmony more agreeable' (other string instruments).

2

HINTS ON ACCOMPANYING

Even before all the figures are learnt—and there is no *continuo* player who is not disconcerted by some passages in J.S.Bach—the accompanist will have seen that the art of accompanying is a subject in itself with its own set of rules, most of them flexible but a few rigid. The function of the accompanist, the number of parts in his chords, what he gives his right hand to do, how he plays the harpsichord, what keyboard idioms he is justified in introducing, how he should conceive his part in aria or recitative, solo or tutti pieces—these problems have various answers, depending on the period, the country, and even the composer concerned. Chapter 2 illustrates from contemporary texts those points of practical importance to the modern player; it does not attempt to answer questions involving the history of harmony as such (for example, whether all pieces in the early seventeenth century ended with a major chord), or those of little significance to the modern player (for example, at what period of time *continuo* players ceased to double fugal entries in upper parts), or those involving wider problems of interpretation (for example, by what period the *concertino* group in a concerto grosso played without harpsichord). Other practical questions that every player needs to ask himself before he accompanies a soloist will be found in the course of Volume Two, the music anthology.

In this chapter, quotation marks (' ') indicate that the advice is quoted verbatim or translated directly from the original; absence of marks indicates that I have expressed the advice implied in the theorist's musical examples or that I have paraphrased remarks in his text. Editorial comment is preceded by the symbol ¶. Each piece of advice must be understood as representing the views of other authors of the date or country, and any opinion that is exceptional or in some way questionable will be observed through comparison with the others. In this chapter I have not pointed out disagreements between authors of different schools—they speak for themselves.

Details of theory-books referred to appear in the Handlist (page 107). Thus 'Geminiani, 1756, II, 1' means 'from F. Geminiani *The Art of Accompaniment,*

Volume II page 1 (London 1756–7)'; the date following the author's name refers to the edition used. In the important cases of Gasparini, C. P. E. Bach and Quantz I have consulted their recent English translations (see Handlist) but have preferred to give the reference to the originals. Volumes of music, as distinct from theory-books, are referred to only in abbreviated form.

1. THE PURPOSE OF CONTINUO

Geminiani, 1755, II, 1

'A good Accompanyer ought to possess the Faculty of playing all sorts of Basses, in different Manners; so as to be able, on proper Occasions, to enliven the Composition, and delight the Singer or Player. But he is to exercise this Faculty with Judgment, Taste and Discretion, agreeable to the Style of the Composition, and the Manner and Intention of the Performer. If an Accompanyer thinks of nothing else but the satisfying his own Whim and Caprice, he may perhaps be said to play well, but will certainly be said to accompany ill.'

C. P. E. Bach, 1762, introduction

'The organ is indispensable [for *continuo*] in church music . . . it provides splendour and maintains order. However, in all recitatives and arias . . . especially those in which a simple accompaniment permits free variation on the part of the singer, a harpsichord must be used. The emptiness of a performance without this accompanying instrument is, unfortunately, made apparent to us far too often . . . Thus, no piece can be well performed without some form of keyboard accompaniment.'

G. B. Fergusio, Motetti, 1612

All chords need not be played, but only those necessary to help the singer.

2. GENERAL ADVICE FOR THE KEYBOARD-PLAYER
Viadana, 1602

'The organist should first look over the piece to be sung, and by noting the nature of the music will always accompany better.'

d'Anglebert, 1689

Keep the hands low; such high chords as those in Example 1 are played only for variety, if the bass line is consistently high.

Example 1

Torres, 1702, 141

'When accompanying do not embellish the part in either hand except with the greatest discretion, for the right will otherwise only confuse the voices (especially if there is only one voice) and the left will otherwise ruin the beat.'

Rameau, 1722, 426 ff.

Note the key of the piece and any change in accidentals. Enter into the spirit of the music or of the words if there are any. If the sound of the harpsichord dies away, repeat the chord on the first strong beat of the bar. Keep the hands in the middle of the keyboard if the bass permits ... 'Nobody knows how to accompany who follows only the figures.'

Geminiani, c. 1745

'Place the Chords between both Hands in such a manner as to produce (by passing from one Chord to another) at once both an agreeable Harmony and Melody. Sometimes playing many Chords, and at other Times few, for our delight arises from Variety ... In swift Movements the Left Hand must strike the plain Notes of the *Bass*, and the Right the Chords, in such a Manner as not to cause a confusion of Sounds, else it will be most prudent to leave out the Chords ... Particular Care should be taken to touch the keys of the Instrument delicately, otherwise the Accompanyment of the *Drum* would be as grateful as that of the *Harpsichord*.'

Bologna, MS L 54, f. 36

'But the most noble advice that one can give oneself is to make a practice of playing from the Full Score [*partitura*] because from that one obtains the surest guide ...'

3. SOME LISTS OF INSTRUMENTS USED (see glossary on page 28)
At the Medici Wedding Celebrations, Florence, 1589
Harps, psalteries (= spinets?), lutes, chitarroni, cittern, mandola, Spanish guitar, Neapolitan guitar, *cembalino adornato di sonagli d'argento* ('little harpsichord adorned with silver bells', probably a type of *arpicordo*, q.v.), a regal and three chamber organs – all used at different moments in the *intermedii*.

E. Cavalieri, Rappresentatione di Anima e di Corpo, 1600, ed. A. Guidotti
Lira doppio, clavicembalo, chitarrone, tiorba – large lira, harpsichord, long-necked lute, bass lute. The instruments may be changed according to the sense of the text – *conforme all'affetto del recitante*. For instance, a sweet-toned organ (*organo suave*) has a fine effect with chitarrone.

C. Monteverdi, Orfeo, 1607
Instruments are changed according to the narration:
    two harpsichords, three chitarroni and harp for the shepherds' dance
    chamber organ and chitarrone for the messenger announcing Euridice's
        death, and for the shepherds' duet-lament following
    regals (alone) for Caronte, bass voice
    two chamber organs and two chitarroni for Orfeo's 'aria' with echoes

Banchieri, 1609, 50–1 (from Agazzari?)
Organ, two harpsichords, three lutes, two chitarroni and two *violoni in contrabasso* (double-basses playing at 16' pitch), heard in church on one Palm Sunday.

Praetorius, 1619, 168ff.; and the motet *Resonet in Laudibus*
Organ, harpsichord or spinet, theorbo, lute, bandora, orpharion, cittern, large lira. When accompanying more than one voice, add a bassoon, dolcian, trombone or, best of all, bass viol (*violone*) to the bass played by organ. In a polychoral piece, a different instrument (organ, regals, harpsichord, lutes) can accompany each choir.

T.Selle, St John Passion, 1643
Organ for chorus, regals for the soloists.

H.Schütz, Mehrchörige Psalmen, 1619; Musikalische Exequien, 1636; Symphoniae Sacrae, ɪɪ, 1647 and ɪɪɪ, 1650; Weihnachtshistorie, 1664
Organ with *Violon* or *Bass-Geige* (gamba, cello).

H.Schütz, Auferstehungshistorie, 1623
The Evangelist can be accompanied by 'a large or small organ, or also by a harpsichord, lute or pandora, according to his choice'.

J.Vierdank, Pavanen, 1637
Clavicymbel, Spinet oder Instrument–harpsichord, spinet or virginals–with theorbo, lute or pandora.

M.Cesti, Il Pomo d'Oro, 1667
Four keyboard instruments and two theorbos; harpsichord for pastoral scene (Act ɪ, Scene 9); regals with trombone and bassoon *continuo* for the underworld scene; viols and chamber organs for Ennone's sleep (Act ɪv Scene 1).

Mace, 1676, 233
The organ for consort music except when the piece is 'airy, jocund, lively and spruce' in which case a harpsichord is better

A.Corelli, trios and solo sonatas, opus ɪ–v, 1681, 1685, 1689, 1692, 1700
Sonate da chiesa: *basso per l'Organo*. Sonate da camera: *violone o cembalo*.

Printz, 1696
Although the *continuo* part can be played by chamber organ, regals, harpsichord, spinet, virginals, lute, theorbo, double harp, large *lira*, pandora and *cither* (cittern), the organ is best–hence the name *bassum pro organo* given to the bass part. The last six instruments add only decorations to the keyboard harmonies.

G. Muffat, Auserlesene Instrumentalmusik, 1701
If the concerto grosso has more than 2–3 players to a part, strengthen the bass line with a large double-bass and 'ornament it with harpsichord, theorbos, harps and similar instruments.'

S. de Brossard, Dictionnaire, 1703 ; *F. Couperin*, Ténèbres, 1714
Harpsichord with bass viol (gamba) or bass violin (cello).

Campion, 1716
The guitar is sufficient to accompany a single voice, but the harpsichord or theorbo is fuller in sound.

North, c. 1726–8 (*Wilson*, 271).
'But I must allow that the attendance of instruments of the *arpeggio* kind, which rattle plentifully, as harpsichords, archlutes [theorbo?] and above all the pandora, give a fullness as well as elegance to the sound, and thereby attract an attention. It is to my knowledge within the memory of man, that in the [then] celebrated consorts divers of the pandoras were used . . .'

Mattheson, 1713, 263; *Mattheson*, 1739, 484
Clavicimbel, Steerstücke oder Flügel–harpsichords of various types are preferable to regals, even in church. A large choir needs two keyboard instruments. Harpsichord with positive organ is a successful combination.

J. S. Bach, performance in 1727
Organ, harpsichord, gambas and lutes in the *Trauerode* at the University Church at Leipzig.

Quantz, 1752, 230; *Choron* and *Fiocchi*, 1804, 35
Harpsichord or pianoforte. One harpsichord for every six *violins* (= violins, violas and cellos?) in the orchestra.

Corrette, 1753
Of the *continuo* group, 'the harpsichord alone has remained as the soul of the harmony, the support and honour of music.'

D. Kellner, 1767, 1
Continuo instruments originally included keyboard, lute, theorbo, *calichon*, pandora, viola da gamba and even guitar; now the chief *continuo* instrument is the keyboard (*Clavier*).

G. M. Telemann, 1773, 16–20
Lute, theorbo, harp, viola da gamba are not as useful as organ and harpsichord (*Flügel*), the latter of which is good in church for recitatives.

28

Bemetzrieder, 1782

Harpsichord or harp.

Türk, 1791

Lute, theorbo, harp, gamba and cello have been known.

GLOSSARY

arpicordo	(i) Small harpsichord, perhaps a pentagonal spinet, (ii) a harpsichord of special construction whereby small metal hooks come into contact with the strings and give it a special *timbre.*
bandora	Same as pandora.
calichon	Small-bodied, long-necked lute.
cembalo	Harpsichord, same as *gravicembalo* and *clavicembalo.*
chitarrone	An important instrument: a bass or arch-lute with long neck, small body and generally wire strings.
cittern	Small plucked instrument with wire strings and a flat back. Of the pandora type of cittern, North wrote 'A sort of double guitar strung with wires, and of those the basses double and twisted, and struck with a quill [plectrum], strangely enriched those vulgar consorts, which now for want of a mixture of the *arpeggio* [instruments playing *continuo*] appear beggarly' (ed. Wilson, page 271).
clavier	Keyboard instrument–possibly, for Kellner, meaning harpsichord.
dolcian	The dulcian, an early type of soft-toned bassoon.
gamba, cello, lirone	In the earlier lists, such string basses are perhaps to be understood as 'ornamental' instruments playing broken chords above the bass line, rather than the single-note bass line itself.
instrument	For many German authors a small, rectangular harpsichord of the type elsewhere called virginals.
lira, lirone, lira doppio	Bowed string instrument often with drone strings (that is, unstopped bass strings); equivalent in early *continuo* to the viola da gamba, its wide finger-board and flatter bridge more easily enabling chords to be played.
mandola	The mandora, a small lute with narrow neck.
orpharion	A smaller-bodied pandora, probably a lute-substitute.
pandora	A bass cittern of characteristic scalloped shape in silhouette; metal strings plucked with a plectrum.

regals *or regal*	A type of organ containing a row of reeds with short, very short or with no resonators. The sound is coarse but fairly strong, the pitch unreliable.
theorbo	Large lute with gut strings and two necks, one of which has frets, the other (with the lower strings) not.
violone	Bass member of the viol family, either what is now called viola da gamba of 8′ (unison) sounding pitch, or a double-bass viol of 16′ (suboctave) sounding pitch. The latter is rarer with the earliest writers. Strictly speaking, *viola da gamba* can refer to any member of the viol family since they are all (except the *violone*) held between or on the legs.

4. TYPES OF ACCOMPANIMENT

Agazzari, 1607, 9

If only one instrument is accompanying, it can be free, 'seasoning the consort' as seems best; but if others are accompanying, the player should regard them closely.

Le Cerf de la Viéville, 1725, i, 297

The best French accompanists avoid the usual faults of Italian *continuo* playing – those unceasing, busy figurations, the broken chords, the ever-rolling arpeggios, the manual display, the disagreement between the harpsichord and bass viol, the chaotic embroidery of both left- and right-hand parts. Such accompaniment serves only to destroy the melody and confuse the singer.

Daube, 1756, 195 ff.

There are three basic types:

'The simple or common': simple 3–4 part chords, left hand having the bass line only.

'The natural': following the mood of the piece, in recitatives or if the singer has a long note. Use arpeggio and broken chords, especially in the right hand.

'The artificial or composite': for pieces with one or a few performers. The right hand can imitate the solo part, adding a second melody below/above the solo line, using embellishments, suspensions, counter-subjects, or enlivening the bass line. J. S. Bach could do this *extempore*, but 'exceptional caution is required'.

5. THE FIGURES

¶ Early figured bass lines are often characterized by 'compound figures' which, either alone (*a*) or with other notes (*b*), indicate the actual pitch of the notes in the right hand:

Example 2 (a) J. Peri *Euridice*   (b) E. Cavalieri *Rappresentatione* p. 10

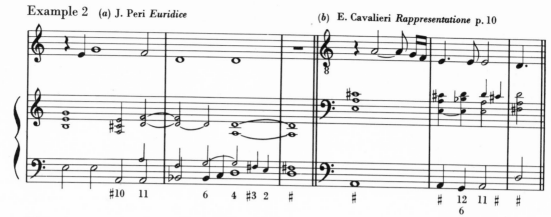

Thus 10 = an octave and 3rd above the bass

    11 = an octave and 4th above the bass

    12 = an octave and 5th above the bass

Figures up to 11 are used in Peri's *Euridice* (1600)

18	Cavalieri's *Rappresentatione* (1600)
14	Caccini's *Nuove Musiche* (1602)
10	Carissimi's *Regeln* (1753 edn.)

'Figures 9–14 are rare – as they should be', according to J. Staden (1626). A few accidentals are the only 'figures' in the bass lines of most early sacred music with *continuo*, such as Viadana's *Concerti* (1602). They can indicate ♭6 and ♯6 as well as ♭3 and ♯3.

A characteristic of later figured basses is the figure written above a rest or during *tasto solo* sections (see §21 below). If the rest is short the player puts a chord on the beat, as in Example 6 below; in other cases he does best by playing no chord at all.

----

6. THE BASS-LINE

Banchieri, Ecclesiastiche Sinfonie, 1607

Do not play the bass with any sort of decoration.

¶ While beginners should follow Banchieri's advice, more experienced players might take note of some later opinions:

The bass line can be varied occasionally (Mattheson, Niedt)

The bass line can be played in another octave (Heinichen)

The bass line can be doubled at the octave (Niedt and others)

The bass note can be repeated if it is long, though this is not necessary on the organ (Kellner)

The right hand takes the chords if the left hand is silent (Mattheson, Telemann)

Gasparini, 1708, ch. 11; *Gasparini*, Cantate, 1695

Do not normally adorn the bass for fear of misleading the harmony and offending the singer. But in music expressing 'unusual sentiments', such a passage as

Example 3

might appear as   or, in quicker tempo,

Example 4   Example 5

Bologna, M S P 134, *c.* 1730, f. 97′; *C. P. E. Bach*, 1762, ch. 37; *Manfredini*, 1775, 59

When the bass rests on the beat, play the chord in the right hand:

Example 6

The last example may sometimes be preferable. If everybody has a short rest (as for fractions of the beat in French Overtures), keep the hands together, the right resting with the left. The beat must be secure, but the player can choose between several possible ways* of accompanying such a bass as:

Example 7

Türk, 1822, 293

Not all quick-repeated bass notes have to be played; they may be omitted or broken:

Example 8

---

*I have not found the third method recommended, but modern players will find it useful in lively
tutti pieces.

¶This last is good advice for the *tutti* sections of early classical symphonies or any other piece where repeated quavers are written rather for cellos and double-basses than for keyboard *continuo*.

———

7. VOLUME ON THE HARPSICHORD

¶The player should remember three facts:

(i) Despite widespread belief to the contrary, a good harpsichord and a good harpsichord-player can distinguish between *loud* and *soft* by means of touch. Loud, firm, detached chords should contrast with soft, caressed, *legato* chords. Changes of registration are a poor substitute.

(ii) Except for a handful of freaks and experimental models, no harpsichord of the figured-bass period had a 16′ stop. During the seventeenth century common specifications were 8′ 4′ (Flemish) and 8′ 8′ (Italian), while a standard eighteenth-century scheme was 8′ 8′ 4′.

(iii) Plectra are important for harpsichord volume. A well-regulated quill will not only give true harpsichord tone of a quality unknown to players of leather-plucked, heavy-bridged, thick-strung, poor-scaled harpsichords, but makes it important to have the right number of parts in a chord. The difference between two, four and six-part chords is understood best—perhaps only—on quill-plucked instruments.

———

Quantz, 1752, 223

The number of parts in a chord depends on the volume required. Four parts are normal, but notes may be added or omitted according to whether:

the harpsichord is weak or strong, its lid open or closed

the other instruments are weak or strong

the harpsichord bass is reinforced by a cello

the piece is 'close wrought' (*forte*) or 'galant' (*piano*)

the listeners are near to or far from the performers.

C. P. E. Bach, 1762, ch. 29, 37, §4

The left hand can take the louder manual, for a good bass line. The player should follow the soloist's crescendo over a long note; he should adjust volume constantly. Give a 'moderately strong attack' when leading other players after a pause.

On the harpsichord, play a chord loudly when (*a*) it is modulating, (*b*) it is on a strong beat in a passage of octaves, (*c*) when the other instruments have a little rest on strong beats, and (*d*) in a recitative, to give the beat before scale-passages and other flourishes:

Example 9

Martini, 1775, II, 114

It is most important to play an unexpected chord (for example, an interrupted cadence) very fully, letting the chord be heard clearly:

Example 10

8. THE NUMBER OF NOTES IN THE CHORDS

Agazzari, 1607; *Bianciardi*, 1607; *Ebner*, c. 1653; *Penna*, 1672

The more voices or instruments being accompanied, the fuller the harmony. Most chords have 3–5 parts.

d'Anglebert, 1689

Six parts for harpsichord, four for organ. Keep the chords in the middle of the keyboard.

Daube, 1756, 200; *Kirnberger*, 1781; *Rameau*, 1722, 426

When filling out chords for accompanying symphonies and concertos, all notes can be doubled except those that are discordant.

9. LEFT-HAND OCTAVES

Agazzari, 1607

Support the voices by occasionally doubling the bass in the lower octave.

Heinichen, 1728, 136

Whenever there is another bass instrument strengthening the bass line, it is better to fill out the chords than merely to double the left hand in octaves.

Quantz, 1752, 236

Octaves are especially good for imitative entries, as in fugues.

Pasquali, 1757; Heck, 1768, 25

Use sparingly, preserving octaves for loud music. Avoid them when the bass line is high.

10. HOW TO USE THE HANDS

¶It is probably fair to say that players must be more careful about spacing and compass when accompanying on the harpsichord than on the piano. Even on modern instruments, the tenor range is nearly always the most effective, though the big arpeggios in recitatives can sweep through several parts of the compass.

Agazzari, 1607; Ebner, c. 1653; Penna, 1672; Albert, 1640; Bologna, MS P140 (7)

'One does well to play within a rather small compass and in a lower register'. Avoid the soloist's note; play below it wherever possible, never above it.

Niedt, 1700, ch. 6

The closer the notes, the better the harmony. Keep the right hand to the compass $c'-c''$, or at most $g-f''$, for the top note of its chords.*

Tosi, 1757, 188

Sometimes follow the voice with the right hand, sometimes play independently; variety is necessary.

Quantz, 1752, 233–4; C. P. E. Bach, 1762, ch. 29, §§ 23–4

Follow the contours of a treble solo (for example, violin) by playing high or low with it; for a bass solo (for example, cello) keep the hands low, even transposing the left hand down an octave. The right hand should never be 'too high', nor obscure the orchestral inner parts.

Kollmann, 1807, 27

Help the singer by giving his note at the top of your chord. But do not be conspicuous in your help; nor is it necessary in *tutti* passages.

---

* Every writer gave a compass, but this is probably the best.

11. DISTRIBUTION OF THE HANDS

¶ For the 'normal' 4-part chords, the left hand plays the bass line only. This was the advice offered to beginners by, for instance, Werckmeister, Holder and d'Andrieu, as it was to the *galant* accompanist of Schröter's and G.M. Telemann's period in Germany. But the better arrangement is two parts in each hand; not only does it encourage good compass and spacing for harpsichord, but bigger chords of 6–8 parts can be more easily incorporated.

Heinichen, 1728, 544 ff.

Give half the notes to the left hand, half to the right; this allows the latter to decorate its part better or even to add a new melody.

Geminiani, c. 1745

'Place the Chords between both Hands, in such a manner as to produce (by passing from one Chord to another) at once both an agreeable Harmony and Melody . . . In swift Movements the Left Hand must strike the plain Notes of the *Bass*, and the Right the Chords . . .'

Mattei, 1788

An accompanist versed in the art of singing will give melodic sense to his right hand, while the left plays the bass, adds middle notes or takes those difficult for the right hand to reach.

12. BREAKING OR EMBELLISHING CHORDS ON THE HARPSICHORD

¶ Harpsichordists can imitate the lute-style at cadences and elsewhere. The French lutenist Perrine decorated Perfect Cadences with passing notes, a lower octave, suspension and a 7th:

Example 11

Mattheson's guide to solo extemporization on the harpsichord (*Grosse General-Bass-Schule*) is largely concerned with broken chords suitable for the keyboard:

Example 12

Such broken chords sound better on the harpsichord if they are sustained or the notes allowed to overlap. This goes for all forms of so-called *Alberti basses*, even those of early Mozart.

Niedt, 1721, 18(*a*); *C.P.E. Bach*, 1762, ch. 29, §17(*b*), ch. 31, §9(*c*)
Broken chords can be employed in both hands: (*a*) in the bass, (*b*) in both hands if volume is required, (*c*) in the right hand for variety of texture:
Example 13

Geminiani, 1756, 1
'The Art . . . chiefly consists in rendering the Sounds of the Harpsichord lasting, for frequent interruptions of the Sound are inconsistent with true melody.' Play 'the several notes whereof the chords consist in Succession'.

13. ARPEGGIO CHORDS

¶ Roger North calls arpeggiation 'the proper genius' of the harpsichord (page 247); like Heinichen (1728) and Mattheson (1731) he takes *arpeggio* to mean 'the breaking of chords, as normally on the harp' that is, broken chords rather than spread chords. It is not always possible to distinguish between the two, but from the beginning players should cultivate as many types of arpeggio as they can—at least six degrees of speeds and violence, with or without diminuendo or accelerando, upwards or downwards. Few *continuo* techniques are as irritating as a constant, unmodified arpeggio. An early direction to play *arpeggiato* occurs in Banchieri's *Organo suonarino* (1638 edition, pages 154–5); a simulated *crescendo* effect seems to be intended:

Example 14

qui pas-cun - tur in li - - - li - is, vul - ne - ra ___

sti cor me - um, vul - ne - ra _____ sti cor me - um,

etc.

Arpeggiato

Penna, 1672, ch. 20

On the harpsichord, chords should be spread *arpeggiare*.

St-Lambert, 1707, 130

Use free arpeggio only in recitatives; otherwise 'break' the chords, keeping to the beat:

Example 15

Türk, 1787, 165

Arpeggios (uncommon on the organ) can be played downwards, upwards, slowly, quickly; or more intricately by repeating various intervals or notes in the chord. Simple accompaniment without embellishment is best; even arpeggio chords can have a bad effect. In recitatives, for instance, avoid them (*a*) if the soloist needs a decisive beat, (*b*) before a modulatory chord which itself should be spread arpeggio:

Example 16   (a) Türk 1822   (b)

Kollmann, 1807, 29

If the harmony has to be continued against a long note, use arpeggio chords.
Various ways of doing this are possible, depending on the music:

Example 17

14. ADDED ORNAMENTS

¶ Adding ornaments to his part is one of the *continuo* player's ways of contributing an interesting realization. Although the earliest writers liked ornaments, most *continuo* of 1750–1800 was extemporized simply, without embellishment; if a composer wanted a fanciful keyboard part, he wrote it out.

Agazzari, 1607; *Banchieri*, 1609, 68–70; *G. Giaccobi*, Salmi, 1609; *Praetorius*, 1619, 116

Trills, slides, trills with turns, *cambiate*, auxiliary notes and *appoggiature* can all be added to the continuo part for variety.

S. Bonini, Affetti, 1615

But do not cover or confuse the singer; avoid all decoration if it has either effect.

Penna, 1672 (*Arnold*, 138)

At a cadence add a trill to either hand or to both hands, singly or at the same time:

Example 18

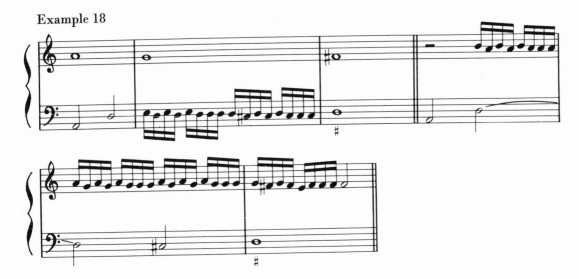

St-Lambert, 1707, 132

On both organ and harpsichord, trills can be added at certain moments, such as an imperfect cadence:

Example 19

but not on the alto G at the same time, as this would be 'too affected'. A trill can also be added to a long-held bass note.

Mattheson, 1731, 323

Trills in both hands are allowed:

Example 20

North, c. 1695 (*Wilson*, 19)

'For an accompanying part which is to maintain the harmony, to trill, and upon the low notes whereon it most leans, unless it be upon a little *ritornello* or solo [for the accompanying instrument], is senseless and destructive to the musick. But that is the fault of our English masters who, accompanying a voice, will clatter trills at the bottom to make one wild. And it is the constant custom of ignorance, to affect superficial ornaments and neglect the substance ...'

Heinichen, 1711, 171 ff.; *Heinichen*, 1728, 583 ff.; *Daube*, 1756, 196 ff.; *D. Kellner*, 1767, 16 ff.*

Trills and mordents enliven the right hand, in any part; they can also be added to the left:

Example 21   J. D. Heinichen, 1728, 547

Bayly, 1771, 58

'Nor ought the accompanist to take more liberty than the singer of introducing his beats [i.e., mordents], trills and flourishes. Not so the two late eminent masters *Greene* and *Handel*; who guided the singer with the most exquisite delicacy, by interspersing such notes only, and those stolen in or whispered as it were by a soft prompture, as might meliorate the harmony, or in emphatic passages give it fulness and dignity, enliven the singer's imagination, and cover any accidental defect ...'

15. ACCIACCATURE

¶The harpsichord's *acciaccatura* is one of its most special effects, useless on piano and organ, but on the harpsichord making quick movements brighter and slow movements richer. The little dissonant notes can be added to quick or slow arpeggios.

Rome MS RI

Fill out the chords in accompanying a soloist. Ignore parallel 5ths and 8ves, but add discordant notes, touching them quickly and releasing them. This effect is called *mordente*.

---

* Heinichen, perhaps due to Italian influence, became more enthusiastic about ornamentation of all types between the writing of his two books (1711, 1728). It is nevertheless certain that the example is intended to illustrate *possible* places for the ornaments, not a literally realized bass.

Example 22 Rome MS RI

Gasparini, 1708, ch. 9

Notes can be interpolated in an *arpeggio* chord, 'especially in recitatives and serious songs.'

Example 23

Such devices can also show 'good taste' in arias and cantatas, but multiple *acciaccature* as (*b*) are rare, being reserved for very affecting pieces:

Example 24

(*a*) (arpeggiated chords)

4

42

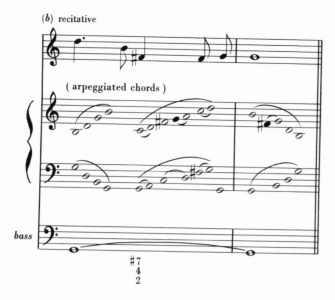

(*b*) recitative

(arpeggiated chords)

bass

d'Anglebert, 1689, 127

Decorate full chords with *acciaccature* and slides, especially those in the middle-to-low part of the keyboard:

Example 25

*Chords 1, 4, and 10 may be intended as descending arpeggios.

Heinichen, 1728, 531 ff.

The device is especially useful for such chords as 6 5 7 6
3 3 5 4
3 2

Example 26

Rameau, 1760, 73–4; *Rousseau*, 1782, 'Acciaccatura'

A note, especially that below the tonic, can be interpolated in arpeggio chords; the Italians play them 'when they want to make more noise.'

    In Italy, *acciaccatura* signifies an inferior note added (from below) to the top or bottom part of an *arpeggio*; in Germany, it is the effect achieved by suspending the dominant over the tonic [= compound *apoggiatura*?]:

Example 27

Geminiani, c.1745, preface; *Geminiani*, 1749, 4

'In accompanying grave Movements, he should make use of the *Acciaccature*, for these rightly placed, have a wonderful Effect. No performer should . . . flatter himself that he is able to accompany well till he is Master of this delicate and admirable secret which has been in use above a hundred years.'

Avison, 1753, 119

'The Use of the *Acciaccatura*, or sweeping of the Chords, and the dropping or sprinkling Notes, are indeed some of the peculiar Beauties of this Instrument. But these graceful Touches are only reserved for a Masterly Application in the Accompaniment of a fine Voice, or single Instrument; and therefore, besides the Difficulty of acquiring a competent Skill in them, they are not required in the Performance of full Music.'

Marpurg, 1756, 70 ff.

Coulé, *arpeggio* and *acciaccatura* can decorate chords:

Example 28 Rameau, 1760

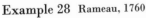

44

Manfredini, 1775, 62

The added notes can be chromatic:

Example 29

16. REPERCUSSION OF CHORDS

Agazzari, 1607; *Albert*, 1640

The harpsichord, harp, theorbo and lute should restrike their chords when necessary, but 'not too often when the voice is singing decorative melodies.' Tied notes can be restruck on the harpsichord, lute and pandora.

Staden, 1626

Do not repeat chords if the singer is good –

G. Caccini, Euridice, 1600

– nor tied bass-notes on every beat. Restrike only when you think right.

Matteis, 1682

On the guitar 'in common time . . . you must give a stroke down of the time of a minim, and two strokes more, the one down, the other up, crotchet time' [A possible interpretation of this, not given by Matteis, is]:

Example 30

 etc.

Geminiani, c. 1745, preface

The harpsichord-player 'now and then should touch the several Notes of the Chord lightly, one after another, to keep the Harmony alive.'

17. WHAT TO DO WITH THE RIGHT HAND

¶ Early composers and writers, such as Viadana, Praetorius and Schütz, assume that the right hand adds passing-notes and decorations (*diminuiren*, diminutions); harpsichord and organ were primarily 'instruments of foundation' but could also take from the 'instruments of ornamentation' such as the lute, certain characteristic figurations, runs, ornamental lines, etc.

Heinichen, 1711, 174–5

A 'slide' or 'transitus' prevents the right hand from leaping from note to note. With passing-notes and slides, such a phrase as (*a*) becomes (*b*) in an *Andante* passage:

Example 31

Heinichen, 1728, 524

Such devices can apply to several parts in the complete texture:

Example 32

C. P. E. Bach, 1762, ch. 32, §12

'Discordant' passing-notes can be added if the harmony is not obscured. Right-hand passing-notes 'provide enticing challenges to an accompanist's inventiveness. But his invention must be in accord with the effect and content of the piece'.

Wiedeburg, 1775, 335

The right hand should aim at a smooth singable progression rather than a new decorative melody of its own:

Example 33

18. EXTEMPORIZED RIGHT-HAND MELODIES

¶This is the most vexed question for the modern player. Although many harpsichordists are too interested in adding their own melody to the composition in hand, it is true that in some circumstances a new theme from the accompanist is desirable. How J.S.Bach accompanied inferior music is reported on page 83; other circumstances giving the player opportunities are the introduction and *ritornello* sections in vocal arias, and the slow movements of instrumental pieces such as violin sonatas. In the arias, however, the most skilful extemporizer should do nothing to distract attention from themes in the bass, since they are being played by a much more melodic instrument than his own: the cello.

Gasparini, 1708, ch. 10; *Gasparini*, Cantatas, 1695
The right hand can decorate its chords, especially when the bass line is simple:
Example 34

But never confuse the singer, nor play his melodic line.

North, c. 1710–20 (*Wilson*, 249)
'It is not allowed a thorough-bass part to break and adorn while he accompanies, but to touch the accords only as may be figured, or the composition requires. Yet there is a difference in the management when the upper parts move slow, and when they divide, or when they are full, or pause. In the latter case, somewhat more airey [i.e., something more melodic] may be put in, and often there is occasion to fill [in the texture] more or less.'

Mattheson, 1719, II ex. 9
For an interesting right-hand part, make use of conventional ornaments (trill, passing-notes, *appoggiature*, slide, mordent, *acciaccature*) and of arpeggio, broken chords and figurations. The best opportunities for extemporizing new melodies in the right hand are

(*a*) against a *cantabile* solo line, whether vocal or instrumental
(*b*) in the sections of an aria where the voice is for the moment not singing.

There is less need for melodic right-hand parts when there is an *obbligato* instrument playing. With ornaments, full chords and a right-hand melody, the following bass line could be interpreted in at least two ways:

Example 35 Heinichen, 1728, 545 ff.

Quantz, 1752, 235

New melodies are effective over repeated chords in *Andante* time:

Example 36 Mattheson, 1731, 360 ff.

Geminiani, 1749

Use arpeggiation, *acciaccature*, ornaments and little melodic figures:

Example 37 (arpeggiated chords)

19. IMITATION

¶Imitating the soloist's thematic material is one of the accompanist's most interesting and challenging practices. He should not, however, rise to the challenge very often for he must remember that such devices can easily disguise or cover up the basic harmony. It was to the lute, one of his 'instruments of ornamentation' not 'of foundation' like the harpsichord, that Agazzari recommended 'imitations on different strings' (*fughe in diverse corde*).

Praetorius, 1619, 137

In solo cantatas, the organist can imitate the soloist's phrase when (*a*) he temporarily rests, (*b*) his runs are followed by plainer notes. In either case, the organist makes his part 'as an echo.'

St-Lambert, 1707, 132

Opportunities will be found, especially in chamber and operatic arias without *obbligato* instruments, for imitation between soloist and the accompanist's right-hand part. This is easier when the soloist's part is printed with the *continuo*.

Example 38 Heinichen, 1728, 579-81

C. P. E. Bach, 1762, ch. 33

There are two kinds of imitation, both usually taking the form of short motifs :

    (*a*) that extemporized by the accompanist in his right hand,

'imitating' the main melody

    (*b*) that extemporized by the accompanist in answer to an improvized

decoration by the soloist:

Example 39

The oblique strokes signify accented passing-notes in the bass.

Tomeoni, 1795, 39; *Drechsler*, 1828, 119

Imitation is frequently no more than decoration of a simple chord, right hand following the left:

Example 40   *right hand*

20. RESTS IN THE SOLOIST'S PART

North, c. 1710–20 (*Wilson,* 249)
Here the accompanist may 'take the liberty to touch with more air [i.e., melody] than is allowed in accompanying' the soloist's melody.

Mattheson, 1731, 290; *Pasquali,* 1757, examples; *C. P. E. Bach,* 1762, ch. 29 §3; *Bertezen,* 1780; the quotation from *Geminiani, c.* 1745, preface
'Whenever the Upper Part stops and the Bass continues, He who accompanies must make some Melodious Variation on the same Harmony, in order to awaken the Imagination of the Performer, whether he Sings or Plays, and at the same Time to give Pleasure to the Hearer.'

21. TASTO SOLO; ALL'OTTAVA

Heinichen, 1728, 515; *Pasquali,* 1757
Tasto solo indicates that the left hand plays the bass alone in single notes, without chords.

Adlung, 1783, 775
Tasto solo indicates that the left hand plays the bass with its octave [above?], but without chords.

C. P. E. Bach, 1762, ch. 22, §5; *Löhlein,* 1791, 84
All'ottava, all'unisono indicate that the bass is played alone with its octave [above?].

Miller; C. P. E. Bach, 1762, ch. 29, §14; *Albrechtsberger,* 1837
If the note is held a long time, restrike it:

Example 41

¶Composers do not necessarily specify *tasto solo* or *all'unisono* when in fact they want it–for example, when all other instruments are playing octaves or unisons together.
C. P. E. Bach (1762, Ch. 22) adds that *all'ottava* is useful for:

    (*a*) 'strikingly expressive' themes in the bass
    (*b*) brilliant themes fashioned from leaps, runs, broken chords, trills
    and other conspicuous motifs.

He also notes that the Italians do not use *tasto solo*; for delicate effects they omit the harpsichord altogether, since otherwise 'they can scarcely play any chord without rolling it.'

22. THEME IN THE BASS
C. P. E. Bach, 1762, ch. 40

Telemann, Graun and J.S. Bach were good at bass themes. If the theme is played by all the instruments in octaves, then play *all'unisono*; if it is figured, chords should be added. So they should if bass instruments alone have the theme below harmony played by other instruments. Good players may improvise a second melody above the bass theme, but only when the soloist pauses or holds long notes.

¶ C.P.E. Bach's last remark seems to advise the accompanist to extemporize a new melody in those introductions to arias in which the given *bass* part has the main theme. (See page 84 in Volume Two.)

-----

23. PEDAL POINTS

¶ Pedal points, like all held notes, should be restruck on the harpsichord at convenient moments—which in recitative would often be between the singer's phrases. In German organ recitative (see below, §27) even the rich discords arising through pedal points might be taken short. In full instrumental pieces, the harpsichord-player will often find that he is most effective in repeating the bass note on the beats, perhaps with mordent. But if the harpsichord is the only accompanying instrument (with cello), the player must play chords and interpret the figures.

C. P. E. Bach, 1762, ch. 24

'The strange figures turn out to be indications of nothing more than ordinary progressions . . . Those who figure them must accept the fact that they will be played *tasto solo* anyway.'

24. PIZZICATO STRINGS
C. P. E. Bach, 1762, ch. 29, §19

'When the bass and several other parts perform their notes *pizzicato*, the accompanist pauses, leaving the passage to the cellos and double basses. But if only the bass is *pizzicato* the accompanist plays his chords, in a *staccato* manner.'

25. RECITATIVE ON THE HARPSICHORD

¶ Some of the techniques already listed, such as right-hand melodies and *tasto solo*, normally arise in the course of accompanying arias and *tutti* pieces; others, such as *acciaccatura* and arpeggio, apply mostly to recitative. Generally speaking, recitative demands even more from an accompanist than does a solo aria, for there is no recurrent beat, the mood is constantly changing (especially in secular cantatas), the cellist has long notes rarely of independent interest, and the harmony requires particularly rich realization. Responding to the singer's mood is the most difficult of these, but C.P.E.Bach's advice (page 55) is useful; so are Tosi's remarks about the types of recitative met with in the period (1757, 150–3):

(*a*) ecclesiastical: the singer should add *appoggiature*, keep the mood serious and the time freer than in (*b*) or (*c*)

(*b*) operatic: a quick, scherzo-like imitation of speech is required

(*c*) chamber cantatas: as if the singer actually meant what he was singing

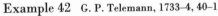

Penna, 1672, 185
Recitatives–'wherein occur many effects through dissonances . . .'

Martini, 1761, f. 21; *J.J. Fux*, Gradus ad Parnassum, 1725, 276
'–not bound to strict harmonic rules.'

St-Lambert 1707, 130–2
At times, having played a long full chord, restrike a single note or two, as if 'the harpsichord were playing itself'; or if suitable, repeat the chord constantly, 'like musket fire' and follow this by a dramatic pause on a 'grand accord.'

Gasparini, 1708, ch. 9
'The more these dissonances can be played full and doubled, the better will be the effect . . . do not annoy or disturb the singer with a continuous breaking of chords, or with ascending and descending scale-passages' . . . Use *acciaccature* of 1 to 4 notes for rich effects. After striking the chord, leave it sounding so that the singer can hear it clearly and sing at his own convenience.

¶The style recommended by some German composers consisted of short chords. In the following example, Telemann advised that at (*a*) the bass is not repeated when the chord is a discord, (*b*) the bass is repeated at resolutions, and (*c*) the final chords be delayed in cantatas until the singer has finished. In operas, where the singer might speak (*spricht*) the last syllables, the final chords can be played in time:

Example 42   G. P. Telemann, 1733–4, 40–1

(a) = do not restrike the bass if the chord is discordant

(b) = restrike the bass for the resolution

(c) = in cantatas, wait and play the cadence after the singer has finished; in operas when the singer speaks
(spricht) the last syllables, do not wait. (Note that there is no letter (c) in b.4)

Quantz, 1752, 238, 272, pl. 23, fig. 5

Keep up the movement–play your final cadence without waiting for the singer
to finish. Help the singer with his notes:

Example 43

Quantz's notation is not clear, but the small notes seem to indicate notes touched (in arpeggio form for the left
hand?) and released. The semibreve G in b.3 is presumably short by one beat.

D. Kellner, 1767, 19–20

Play different types of arpeggio depending on the mood of the piece. Often the
voice leaves a discord unresolved, in which case the keyboard should resolve it:

Example 44 [P.W.]

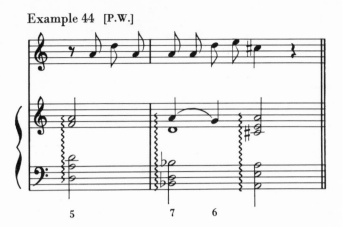

C. P. E. Bach, 1762, ch. 38

'An accompanist must be watchful. He must listen constantly to the principal performer . . . he must never desert the singer. When the declamation is rapid, the chords must be ready instantly . . . without arpeggio. Arpeggios find their natural employment in quite different situations: in slow recitatives and in pieces with sustained chords played by other instruments. As soon as the accompaniment moves from sustained to short detached notes, the accompanist must play detached resolute chords, unarpeggiated, and fully held by both hands. Even if the part is notated in tied white notes [semibreves], the keyboardist should play detached. A heavy attack is most necessary in the theatre . . . When a singer departs from the written notes, it is better to strike the chord repeatedly than to play isolated notes.'

¶It is uncertain when German accompanists began to play recitative chords short, either on organ or harpsichord; but see below, §27.

––––––––––

Rousseau, 1782, 'Accompagnement'

In Italian *recitativo secco* [in opera buffa, intermezzi, etc.] play each chord fully but only once; do not restrike or rearpeggiate unless the strings are also accompanying. Play the chords short and add no ornaments. The Italians like to hear nothing from the accompaniment in such recitative (*Les Italiens ne veulent pas qu'on entende rien dans l'accompagnement*). But for French recitative [and for opera seria] sustain the chords, arpeggiate gracefully and continually from top to bottom, and fill out the sounds as you can.

Pasquali, 1757, pl. 27

In recitative the harmony is to be filled up as much as possible. Spread the chords, whether the text is 'common, tender or passionate'. For anger or surprise, use little or no *arpeggio*, both hands striking 'almost at once'. The last chords should be abrupt if the sense is at an end.

Example 45 Pasquali

written

played

Da-mon who long a - dor'd this sprightly Maid, yet ne-ver durst his love re-late, re-solv'd at last to try his fate. He sigh'd, she smil'd, He kneel'd and pray'd, She frown'd, He rose and walk'd a - way But soon re-turn-ing look'd more gay, and Sung and danc'd, and on his Pipe, a cheerful Ec-ho play'd.

abrupt

Löhlein, 1791, 183–4

If the recitative is quick–for a section or as a whole–do not break or spread the chords. Do not overuse the arpeggio. Give the singer's note on the top of your chord.

Example 46

*At this point Löhlein gives the r.h. a B, but it is best omitted.

5

nicht? du nimmst ihn nicht? Wohl-an, dein Wil-le soll ge-schehn

Ah my Emmanuel! there he lies, bowed deeply in the dust. Struggling against death, he looks towards Heaven and cries aloud:
'Father, let this hour be passed! Take the bitter cup away from my mouth. You do not take it? Ah, so your will be done.'

Kollmann, 1807, 27, 30

The harpsichord player need not sustain chords: notes written as o or ♩ can be played ♩𝄽 :

Example 47

etc.

Türk, 1822, 301 ff.

Help the singer by being careful to touch his note:

Example 48

A great deal depends on the keyboard-player in recitative. He should contribute to the expressiveness of the piece. If other instruments are accompanying, play in strict time, avoiding arpeggio whenever the chord is in any way decisive.

Example 49

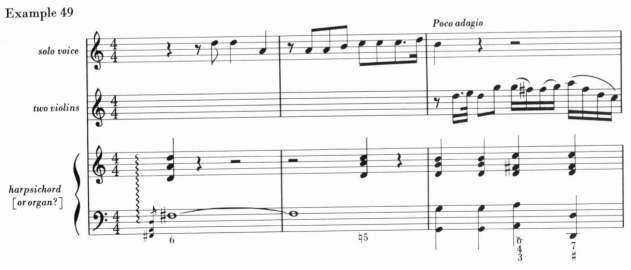

*The arpeggio appears to tell the player to restrike the chord.

26. CONTINUO ON THE ORGAN

¶Organists are generally advised to play with extreme discretion: four-part chords, tied notes where appropriate, and a soft registration. Recitative on the organ is a subject in itself (see §27); so is registration. But the following remarks can serve as introduction to a technique that is basically much simpler than the harpsichord's. The restrained style of many early seventeenth-century motets, whether with one singer or four singers, requires delicate registration. Viadana (1602) and Gasparini (1708) both direct that full passages can be accompanied by large chords (played by hands and feet) but with no extra stops added. Players will find this good advice for such pieces as Carissimi's oratorios, where choruses and solo recitatives-arias alternate. The Germans, on the other hand, liked more stops drawn when the music was full; D. Speer (1697) recommends that the principal 8′ (Open Diapason) and Mixture be added. Organists in central Europe drew strong stops for the bass.

C. Monteverdi, Magnificat, from the *Vespers*, 1610

Vary the registration from *Principale* (Open Diapason) to *Principale, Ottava e Quintadecima* (Diapason, Principal 4′, Fifteenth 2′) and so to *organo pleno* (full Great chorus, no reeds or 16′ stops).

Praetorius, 1619, 138, 116

If there are two manuals, prepare one louder than the other, for dynamic changes. Decorate the part if the registration is bright.

Schütz, Auferstehungshistorie, 1623

The choir should be positioned near the organ, which need have no more than four stops. A quiet Gedackt 8′ is used, the pedal added only for tutti passages.

Samber, 1707, 150–1.

Stopped Diapason 8′ + Flute 4′ for manuals. Posaune 8′ + Oktave 8′ + Quinte 5⅓′ for pedals, when accompanying several instruments. Subbass 16′ + Fagott 8′ for pedals in *tutti* passages.

Werckmeister, c. 1715

The organ *continuo* requires few embellishments. Play simply, especially if the singers or players have florid parts. A typical layout for organ is:

Example 50

Niedt-Mattheson, 1721, 102 ; *C. P. E. Bach*, 1762, ch. 29 ; *Adlung*, 1783, 587–9
If the choir is large, use Prinzipal 8′ (Open Diapason) and pedal Subbass 16′. If the bass part is difficult, play it on the manual: Quintadena 16′ or Bourdon 16′ with Prinzipal 8′ is suitable.

Avison, 1753, 121ff.
In concerti grossi, the organist plays mostly *tasto solo*, though he can double the main theme when it appears. The organ part 'should never be struck in Chords with the Right Hand, as upon the Harpsichord, but in all the full Parts, the leading Subject should be singly touched, and the Performer proceed through the rest of the Movement with the Left Hand only.'

Schröter, 1772, 187 ff.
Prepare a soft manual for sudden *piano* changes. Do not use 16′ manual tone: it thickens the harmony. Combine 8′ and 4′ stops. For an aria with one or two *obbligato* flutes and muted strings, the organ can imitate the effect as follows:

Flutes: Great Organ, Flauto traverso 8′ + Gemshorn 8′ (right hand)
Accompaniment: Choir Organ, Quintadena 8′ + Gedackt 8′ (left hand bass and chords)
Bass line: Pedals, Violon 16′ + Prinzipal 8′, without manual coupler

Bédos de Celles, 1770, iii, 533
Combine as many 8′ and 4′ stops as are necessary for good support–but no more.

27. GERMAN RECITATIVE ON THE ORGAN

¶The problem here concerns the custom, widely established by 1750 or so in Protestant Germany, of playing short chords in church recitative. To play crotchet chords followed by rests, no matter how the composer actually notated the bass, was 'one of the organist's most important rules', according to the influential D. G. Türk (1787, 162–4). Schröter gave a similar rule but thought the left hand should sustain the bass line, though not the chords above. When the convention arose is uncertain. Niedt's remark (see below, 1721), does not apply to recitative, but the criterion for all organ-playing is obviously to be discreet. Short chords gave maximum clarity to the singer's words–very important with the Biblical and meditative texts of cantatas and Passions. Schütz in his last 'oratorios' thought that there need be no organ at all for the recitatives, the old plainsong (*choraliter*) style being suitable. For the sake of variety, several of J. S. Bach's Leipzig cantatas have one or more recitatives written with short bass notes; so do the *continuo* parts of the *St Matthew Passion*, although the score contains the conventional long, tied notes familiar in, for example, the *Christmas Oratorio*.

Schütz, Auferstehungshistorie, 1623

The narrator's recitative can be accompanied by chamber organ, or by a harpsichord with lute, pandora, etc. according to taste. The organist should remember to decorate his part with runs and embellishments whenever the singer holds or repeats a single note (*in einem thon weret*).

Heinichen, 1711, 226

Play without arpeggios, sustaining each chord until the next one. But hands can be lifted after a new chord, especially if the sustained organ-sound becomes irksome, as it might when a note is held for 3 or 4 bars. The singer must be heard.

Niedt-Mattheson, 1721, 121

Do not sustain full organ (with reeds) for more than a beat or two, even when the orchestra contains trumpets and drums.

Voigt, 1742, 57

Lift the hands and let the singer be heard.

D. Kellner, 1737, 19 ff.

Play the bass note also on the pedals if the bass is weak. The chords may be held, if desired, in *recitativo stromentato*; but if the bass has very long notes, take off the hand and pause until the next chord, so that the singer can be heard distinctly.

Hahn, 1751, 57

On the organ avoid *arpeggio* and lift the right hand [but not the left?] until the next chord is played.

C. P. E. Bach, 1762, ch. 38, §5

'In recitatives with sustained accompanying instruments [*arioso* and *stromentato*] the organ holds only the bass, the chords being lifted soon after they are played. Organs are seldom purely tuned, with the result that held chords, which are often chromatic in such recitatives, would sound ugly . . .'

Petri, 1767, 42–4

'The organist takes his chords short, neither sustaining them nor dragging the notes except where *tenute* is written above a note or when it is particularly long'. 8′ Gedackt (Stopped Diapason) is probably sufficient for accompanying recitative, but another 8′ stop may be added, as might a second 16′ stop for the pedals. But soft when the singer enters! The organist may use broken, arpeggio or 'dismembered' (*zergliederten*) chords, but no trills. Often the bass line is sustained alone, on manual or on pedals.

Türk, 1822, 299 ff.

Avoid arpeggio, raising the right hand–or both hands–unless *tenuto* tells you otherwise.

Performance of a cantata *Lobet ihr Knechte des Herrn*, page in a
family album of *c.*1775 (Nürnberg, Germanisches Museum).
Three singers or boy trebles are accompanied by strings, wind
and brass instruments, with a *continuo* group, the whole directed
by a conductor with a scroll in his hand and, it seems, performing before an audience in a tavern or music-club. The cantata
has a sacred text but since the performance is not in church, a
harpsichord is suitable. One interesting detail is that the bass
string instrument has its own part, something rarely shown in
contemporary pictures.

3

CHANGING STYLES OF ACCOMPANIMENT

A good Accompanyer ought to possess the Faculty of playing all sorts of Basses, in different Manners. . . . F. Geminiani *The Art of Accompaniment* 1756

All the chords found in the period of figured bass were described in Chapter 1 and few players are likely to discover any other chords, even in the more complex compositions of Purcell and J.S.Bach. But Chapter 2 must be regarded as little more than an introduction to the art of accompaniment. Among the requirements of a *continuo* player only a knowledge of figured chords and methods of playing them can be learnt from books; other duties, such as directing, supporting, controlling and even inspiring the other performers, cannot. A simple musical event like a change of speed—

Example 1

—might be listed by D.G.Türk as something to watch and to be prepared for; but, unlike *acciaccature*, harpsichord touch, or extemporized right-hand melodies, it cannot properly be defined, described or illustrated. A student could assimilate all the advice given in Chapter 2 (mostly by second-rate composers, unfortunately), play all the exercises in Volume Two, and yet feel entirely lost the first time he played *continuo* with an orchestra; if at the same time he were trying to direct from the keyboard, replacing the conductor in a small ensemble, he would do far more harm than good.

Many *continuo*-players forget that they are first and foremost accompanists, and prefer to fill the air with a *perpetuum mobile* of harpsichord tinklings, seeking opportunities for clever imitations, 'improving' the piece with their own ideas instead of closely supporting the soloist in his. The duty of accompanying demands different things at different times: to accompany means much more than to efface oneself, and indeed rarely means that at all. Chords must be correct; but sometimes the piece demands block chords in the right-hand, sometimes an extemporized melody, sometimes a simple unobtrusive part, sometimes a louder and more complex part, even at times a temporary 'disagreement' with the soloist. There are times in Handel's Italian cantatas or Biber's violin sonatas, for example, when the accompanist does best by following the soloist's soft, lyrical melody with stern chords, or by interrupting his violent phrases with gently flowing chords. This requires much experience, but is by no means unattainable. On the other hand, many keyboard-players who respond to the often carefully specified effects in Schubert's piano accompaniments will be heard to accompany Caccini as if he wrote primarily to give them an opportunity to show how lavishly they can decorate root-position triads.

All too often, it is only fair to say, modern realizations of figured bass have to be largely guess-work. Descriptions of the original accompaniment to early monody are too vague for the player, although they may satisfy the historian; in other cases, such as the recitatives in J.S.Bach's mature cantatas, it is difficult to reconcile the different evidence from equally 'authentic' sources. Nevertheless, it is possible to generalize about the varying styles of accompaniment, to trace the outlines of the main 'schools' of *continuo*-playing to which every piece played by a modern accompanist can be expected to belong.

THE EARLIEST BASSO CONTINUO

Basso continuo was a notational device with two purposes:

(i) As the organ part in concerted church music it took the form of an 'abbreviated full score' whereby the organist played the lowest bass note at each point, together with its inferred or assumed chord. In polychoral pieces, the bass line might be 'extracted' from the several vocal bass lines (as in A. Striggio's 40-part motet *Ecce beatam lucem*, MS of 1587) and often more than one bass line was printed for the organist or organists. Actual figures were rare in church music before well into the seventeenth century, the organist either readily understanding the harmony or playing wrong chords, as the case may be; accounts of the latter are not rare. In most major churches of Spain and Italy the organists are likely to have accompanied vocal polyphony during much of the sixteenth century. By 1600 in Madrid and 1608 in Venice, works of Victoria and Palestrina were being published with an organ *continuo* part (Palestrina's *Motectorum Quinque Vocibus . . . addite parte infima pro pulsatoris Organi comoditate*) and many Italian and a few German composers were prefacing their works between 1600 and 1630 with hints on playing their figured, semi-figured and unfigured bass parts. It is clear that *basso continuo* lines were less troublesome for both composer and player than either a fully written-out transcription (*intavolatura*) or a full-score copy of a many-voiced composition (*partitura*). One of the first figured-bass theorists, Lodovico da Viadana (1602), justified his bass part on the grounds of its being less troublesome to write. Viadana's remarks were known to the German theorist and critic Praetorius, who also quoted from the preface written by B. Strozzi to a collection of church music:

> with the aid and practice of these figures, organists arranged and
> performed Palestrina's motets . . . in such a way that it seemed to
> listeners as if the pieces were written in full tablature. *Syntagma*
> *Musicum*, iii, 134

–that is, a literal transcription on two staves. To these ends composers had different means, as Banchieri noted in 1609; some printed a bass line with the treble part above, some gave the bass line alone or with accidentals to show some of the chords.

(ii) *Basso continuo* also denoted the bass line of harmonies extemporized by instruments in secular entertainments–harmonies supporting freely measured song-recitation or *recitativo*. Though neither codified nor published, *basso continuo* as a practical device may well be older for secular music than for sacred. Castiglione wrote in 1528 that he liked best 'singing to a lute and reciting [*per recitare*] which lends such beauty and effect to the text',[1] although nobody knows when this 'reciting' may have taken the form of a free melody above a bass-line, figured or unfigured. In A. Doni's *Dialogo* of 1544, poems were recited to some sort of music played by *viuola* or *lira*, although it is not clear whether this music provided simple background sounds or whether it was a properly extemporized accompaniment to the poems.[2] Amateur musicians like Castiglione and Doni often use terms in a misleading way. Both authors were associated with Florence where secular entertainments on such occasions as weddings brought together vocal and instrumental music, verse and dancing, and resulted in a rich and mature 'operatic' orchestral sound: *continuo* groups plus string-and-wind accompaniment plus *obbligato* solo instruments. One Medici wedding of 1565 had an entertainment of Amor and Psyche in which the music 'was played by a consort of four harpsichords of large compass [*gravicembali doppi*], two lutes, two violins [? *viole d'arco*], two trombones, two tenor recorders, one transverse flute and a *cornetto muto*.'[3] From at least 1597, the published *basso continuo* of such works as Peri's operas, Caccini's songs and Cavalieri's sacred dramas was a bass line figured more systematically than that of contemporary sacred music and allowing one or more instruments to play the chords according to their nature and according to the *rubato* methods of the singer. A written-out accompaniment would not only have been unsuitable for the several instruments reading the part—organ, harpsichord, double-bass and organ in Cavalieri's *Rappresentatione* (1600)—but would have contributed a rhythmic rigidity unsympathetic to the singer's free line. The affecting expressiveness of this free line was, after all, the nature and purpose of operatic monody and recitative.

The difference in aim between these two early types of *continuo* should show itself in the way the player interprets his part. Generally, this difference holds good throughout the whole figured-bass period. The measured full texture of sacred choral music should be accompanied on the organ in simple four-part style, with or without pedal (depending on the difficulty of the bass-line); the organ either duplicates the vocal lines or, if the piece is a solo, supplies such parts as might have been sung if the piece were choral. The unmeasured solo recitative of early opera and oratorio should be accompanied by harpsichord and/or other instruments in a constantly changing style and texture, now thin, now full, forceful or gentle, depending on the text and the singer's method. As the earliest composers and theorists saw, both types are best served by a further bass instrument: string or, less commonly, brass and woodwind. This instrument used the same copy as the keyboard-player, judging by drawings and paintings of the period.

Monodic music of a more measured type knew no boundaries. *Stilo recitativo* soon became popular in church—not so much in the liturgical movements of mass and motet as in sacred or devotional pieces such as the oratorios and Passions in 'popular' services at certain times of the year. Conversely the 'full style' of instrumental and vocal music became familiar in opera, especially the orchestral overture, *ritornello*, and dance. The most difficult (and interesting) duty for the *continuo* player was and still is the recitative, a close second being the solo aria without *obbligato* instrument.

Since *continuo* players of monodic music extemporized above a bass in a way suitable to the technique of their particular instrument, modern players have to follow their own technique and experience. Models for realizations do exist, but they are to be treated with caution. In Example 2, a madrigal of Luzzaschi (*a*) and a theory-book model by Schütz (*b*) are realized for keyboard instruments without any of the freedoms which were normally taken in recitative by such instruments as lute and chitarrone; only the essential keyboard harmonies are given, suggesting a very plain accompaniment. On the other hand, it may be 'correct' to realize the contrapuntal potential of Viadana's solo *concerti* in the way suggested by one recent scholar (*c*).[4] In such music, the *continuo* player has many opportunities for imitating the soloist.

Example 2 (a) Luzzaschi

(c) Viadana

written

Hunc pre-cla-rum di - em,   hunc__ pre-cla-rum di - em   per or-bem ter - ra - rum   de-vo-

accomp.

ta so-lem-ni-ta - te   ce-le-bre - mus   de-vo - ta so-lem-ni-ta - te   ce-le-bre-mus

For later advice on recitatives, see Chapter 2. Here it is enough to note that harmonic licence often arose through the relationship of voice to instrument – in the Schütz example, the organ right hand simplifies and 'disagrees' with the voice. A harpsichord and lute sustaining or restriking their triads in Example 3 would bring out the dissonance of the solo line as it suspends a note from the previous chord, anticipates the next, causes a false relation, or simply juxtaposes one $\frac{5}{3}$ chord to another.[5]

'Softening' the voice's dissonances by giving the accompanist extra notes, which reconcile his triad to the vocal line (as in a recent edition of Monteverdi's *Orfeo*), totally destroys the intended effect. Although the player must not play so many arpeggios and repercussions that the singer is irritated, what does matter is that

Example 3   Monteverdi *Orfeo*, Act IV

*Probably a violin

he let his chord be heard clearly enough to bring out any harmonic clashes. In instrumental music generally, such as the early violin sonatas, the *continuo* player can possibly afford to be a little more independent–but not much more.

BASSO CONTINUO OF THE LATER SEVENTEENTH CENTURY

German church music of this period, including the 'oratorios' of Schütz, the cantatas of Buxtehude and the chorales of every Lutheran composer, requires a somewhat simpler technique than that for the earlier Italian music. *Continuo* players should study the examples given by Agazzari (Example 4) for playing the cantatas or motets with instrumental accompaniment of such composers as Praetorius and Schütz.[6]

Example 4

(a) Agazzari

(i)   (ii)

Agazzari's note:

(i) Passing-notes in the bass: the right hand holds the chord

(ii) Contrary motion

(iii) Should the bass leap, keep the right hand smooth by playing adjacent chords

(iv) Not passing-notes in the bass: harmonize with different chords.

The bass line is the *bassus generalis* part of Praetorius' *Wir glauben all'*, pt. II, from *Polyhymnia* (Wolfenbüttel 1619), a polychoral piece for three choirs and instruments. This part is not always the lowest of the four bass parts.

Although the style is simple here, the harmony is occasionally doubled and decorated. An even plainer style may be appropriate for late Schütz, though not for his earlier motets. Werckmeister (1698) went so far as to suggest that figures were a guide to what organists should *avoid*: in the suspension $^{5}_{4}$ $^{5}_{3}$, for example, he should not double the 4th if the singer has it, but play the 5th only. In German chamber music, the accompanist should bear in mind the style imitated by the composer–Italian or French–and accordingly play his part more freely, especially on the harpsichord, for which few German figured-bass books were written.

For Italian chamber music of this period, most notably the solo violin sonata and the trio sonata, a fuller, more flamboyant style is in keeping. Although the solo parts do not require intricate counterpoint or even arresting melodies from the harpsichordist, they do require full chords and strong rhythms.[7]

Example 5   Corelli, opus V no. 1, realized by G. Antoniotto and earlier writers (c. 1700)

*Corelli's sign: it is omitted by Antoniotto

Beginning of 4th movement

Corelli, opus V no. 3, part of 2nd movement   and part of last movement

Whether composers approved of players changing the bass, as Antoniotto changed Corelli's bass in these fragments, is another question; none of the alterations are improvements. What is certain, however, is that modern players should not use a 4′ stop on harpsichord or organ for this particular texture. The 'Italian *continuo* harpsichord' as a recognizable type had two sets of strings only, both 8′; many instruments indeed could not play them singly. The high position of the right hand in such passages as Example 5 is based on the assumption that both 8′ ranks be used together, without 4′. The modern player is best advised to avoid all 4′ (and of course 16′) strings, with two exceptions: (i) in tutti passages of choral or instrumental pieces, such as choruses in opera and oratorio, French suites, *ritornello* sections of Italian concertos; and (ii) when his instrument's 8′ ranks are so feeble (probably leather-plucked) that the brightness of the 4′ is essential. In the latter case, the right hand should remain below c″, taking chords lower spaced than those in Example 5.

Similarly in the slow movement of the Vivaldi concerto (Example 6), the *continuo* organ alone accompanies the soloist, and its chords are written for a single 8′ stop. The registration is not specified but can be assumed to be in accordance with organ-practice of the time.[8] If no organ were available, the accompaniment could be played on harpsichord, the right hand preferably an octave lower.

Example 6   *Grave*

THE MATURE ITALIAN BASSO CONTINUO STYLES

From a study of the small treatises of L. Penna, A. Scarlatti, B. Pasquini, F. Gasparini, F. Geminiani, N. Pasquali, G. Antoniotto, V. Manfredini, and several anonymous manuscripts, and by playing the extant *basso* realizations to Scarlatti's cantatas,[9] the player can build up a picture of two well-developed styles of accompaniment that influenced players inside and outside Italy.* The 'Scarlatti cantata' style consisted of fairly smooth melodic lines, often imitative, usually in few parts, and somewhat resembling Heinichen's example of harpsichord imitation (page 49); the other style was characterized by homophonic chords of many parts (the basic texture in Manfredini's *Regole* is five, that of Corsini MS R I six parts), full or in arpeggio form, with slides and *acciaccature* which were often highly dissonant. Such richness of style may be thought a compensation for the

---

*Many Italian and Spanish MSS are not yet listed and some important figured-bass treatises may still await discovery.

simplicity of the harmony it clothed, for even the simplest progressions were an opportunity for six-part chords, double passing-notes and repeated discords (Example 7). The examples in the Corsini MS are apparently formulae to be learnt as such.

Example 7   Realization

*l.h. chord, original middle note B not C

Gasparini (1708) believed that anyone who had heard his master Pasquini had enjoyed

> ... the truest, most beautiful and noble manner of solo and *continuo* playing; and with this full, rich style you hear from his harpsichord a perfection of marvellous harmony;

but Mattheson, who seems to have heard Pasquini accompanying no less a soloist than Arcangelo Corelli,[10] did not report anything remarkable, except that a theorbo joined the harpsichord for the *continuo* part. Even so cosmopolitan a German as he let slide an opportunity to recommend the full harpsichord style which would have been a revelation to him and which influenced his own *General-Bass-schule*. Example 8 is part of a song interpreted by an Italian composer in the idiomatic keyboard style, from the same source as Example 7.

Example 8

written

Son un cer - to ___ spi - ri - tel - - - lo che do'a

played

tut - ti ___ nell' a - mo - re ___ ma più mo - ti ho nel cer - vel -

- - lo ___ ch'o - ri - ol* nel bat - ter ___ l'ho - re

etc.

* Old word for 'orologio'

two later extracts

Col mar - tel dell' em - pie - ta - de

The small dissonant notes or *acciaccature* are so remarkable that other characteristics may be missed:

- (i) the whole is probably to be played *arpeggiando*
- (ii) the right hand follows the melody fairly closely for the first strain, then lowers its ambit
- (iii) the left hand fills in but avoids low 3rds
- (iv) the simple rhythm is nowhere disguised
- (v) the hands are close together and cadences allow the richest chords
- (vi) full chords thin out when quavers appear in the bass

Rameau (1760) not only associated the *acciaccatura* with the Italians but noted that by then they generally played without arpeggio: the sharp effect was not mollified by spreading the chord. It is perhaps unnecessary to add that such style suits neither the piano nor (as Gasparini admitted) the organ.

The richness of the idiom no doubt depended on who was playing. Milder textures can be found in such written-out accompaniments as Gasparini's for his own cantatas (see below, Example 17) or that for a sonata *per viola da gamba ou viola da braccio* ascribed, in two different MSS, to Handel or 'Hendel' (Example 9). Here the Italian style admits of various textures resulting in an idiom rather more difficult to improvize than the examples above.[11] But for Italian cantatas, recitatives and much instrumental music, the richest style is usually appropriate.

Example 9   G. F. Handel

THE MATURE FRENCH BASSO CONTINUO STYLE

French accompanists seem to have exploited the harpsichord richly in their realizations, but without undue extravagance. One writer reported in 1725 that

> usually all that is heard in Italian music is a *continuo* accompaniment
> varied without respite, the manner of decorating the chords often taking
> the form of arpeggio and figurations. This pulls the wool over the eyes
> of those who know nothing better . . . 12

and clearly the Italian technique would be out of place in a gentle recitative or in a lyrical violin movement. St-Lambert was the first theorist who took pains to

Example 10   J. H. d'Anglebert

give advice to the *accompanist,* as distinct from the soloist or elementary figured-bass student: much of his treatise is concerned with the relationship of accompanist to soloist, rather than the method of playing chords as such. Modern players who have worked on French harpsichords of the period will not be surprised that in their examples the better theorists laid emphasis on the rich tenor and bass range of the instrument. Example 10 contains two interpretations of a figured bass by J.H.d'Anglebert, the second of which incorporates arpeggio, *acciaccature* and *coulés.*

A written-out version of the latter appears on page 42. The lower spacing of the chords and the more restrained use of non-harmonic notes distinguishes this style from the Italian, as does the subtlety of conception implied by the general advice of St-Lambert and Boyvin. Example 96 in Volume Two demonstrates the French *obbligato* style—less rich, but suitable for much of the nondescript music found throughout Europe in the 'late baroque' period. Charm, if not musical power, is increased by such delicate accompaniment, as can be seen in much of La Barre's realized basses.

GERMAN CONTINUO STYLE IN THE EARLY EIGHTEENTH CENTURY

The German Empire was a very large area divided into states with fairly individual cultures, and it is not to be imagined that one single *continuo* style can be discerned—that a cantata of 1700 in Hamburg was accompanied in the same way as an opera of 1720 in Vienna. In most churches the organ reigned supreme, although in some a large lute or theorbo was still to be heard in the 1720s. For sacred concerts, such as the Lübeck *Abendmusiken,* a harpsichord might be used for *continuo,* from about 1730 onwards; but how exceptional was this?

Some experienced and authoritative German writers appear to have approved of using a harpsichord in church: Praetorius, Schütz, Mattheson and C.P.E. Bach. But there are special circumstances behind their respective suggestions. Like so many writers, they had their own particular needs in mind: Praetorius was conscious of his Italian models, Schütz of the cosmopolitan court at Dresden; Mattheson was a wealthy amateur in Hamburg, C.P.E.Bach was writing for the *galant* music of Berlin. Furthermore, St Thomas, Leipzig, like a few major churches throughout north and central Germany, did own a harpsichord and had it kept in the west gallery near the singers. This and other evidence, such as non-transposed figured *continuo* parts for a few cantatas (the high-pitched organ needed a transposed part) also suggest that J.S.Bach did make use of a harpsichord. He may well have used it in exceptional circumstances, or at home, in rehearsal, in the *collegium musicum* meetings, perhaps for the Latin motets in the chief Lutheran Services; he may even at times have sat at the harpsichord and accompanied recitatives from the full score, allowing organist and bellows-blower a short respite. But for normal Sunday cantatas, Good Friday Passions, festival Magnificats and German funeral motets, the *continuo rested entirely with organ and string bass*. Some of the arguments for this generalization are as follows: (i) with a few exceptions, these works had a figured-bass part transposed for organ, even for those secular pieces used in church cantatas (for example, the movement from Brandenburg Concerto No. 1 in Cantata No. 52); (ii) a few typical parts are in fact labelled *organo*–players, builders and writers in central Germany assumed that the *Rückpositiv* (the little organ in the front of the gallery, as at St Thomas) was placed there for *continuo* purposes; (iii) attractive though it might be both to us and to the old courtly circles of Praetorius and Schütz, the use of harpsichord *and* organ in the same work was unlikely in the Leipzig of 1730, nor was it probable in Saxony at that period that the *director musices* (J. S. Bach) himself contributed to the *continuo*; (iv) no harpsichord high up in the gallery of a gothic hall-church would have the slightest effect below, especially when it was small–as was the instrument in St Thomas, called *spinet* in some sources.

In England, Handel had a more interesting *continuo* group for his theatre oratorios: two harpsichords and two chamber organs for *Esther* (1732), *Deborah* (1733), and *Saul* (1738); one harpsichord and one organ (perhaps a composite *claviorgan*) for other works. Harpsichord was used for recitatives and most arias, organ for choruses and a few arias: the contrast was simple, especially as the organ very often played *tasto solo* only, and its chords had four simple parts, judging by the little organ coda to the chorus 'Doleful tidings' in *Esther*. In German chamber music, *Flügel* or *Klavier* usually indicated harpsichord, although the general impression is that chamber organs were as active in secular music and as common as comparably-priced harpsichords. From at least 1750 the pianoforte sometimes replaced the harpsichord, notably in the music of modern composers like C. P. E. Bach and Quantz (who recommended it for *continuo* work). For string concerti grossi, which always imitate Italian styles more or less, two harpsichords are desirable for full-dress performances, though no doubt on many occasions there would have been only one available. That Avison (1753 edition, page 117), a late theorist, thought the harpsichord should be silent in the *concertino* sections and join in only during the *tutti*, indicates the move towards a simple *continuo*.

German theory-books more and more advocated simple *continuo* in four parts. F. W. Marpurg complained that all anyone could learn from them was 'the purity of four-part chords' and nothing of 'the art and taste of accompaniment'.[13] But four parts are ideal for beginners. Even for experienced players, such simple chords have two virtues: they are rhythmically secure, and they are also suitable for music that is harmonically simple–such as that written by J. S. Bach's younger contemporaries. Most players would probably prefer Heinichen's 'full-voiced' chords of five and six parts to his examples in four, as they would probably prefer for Corelli's sonatas the Italian kind of realization shown in Example 5 to the simple harmonization made by one German contemporary (MS now in Berlin, B.B. Mus. MS theor. 348). But playing in only four parts is sensible for beginners, just as for certain music it is the most 'authentic' style.

Evidence for Bach's own realizations is at first glance conflicting, but it does reflect what might be called the double German character of strict simplicity and virtuoso extravagance. The reports show him to have been an exceptionally vivid accompanist:[14]

> Anyone who wants to have the right idea about what refinement in continuo-playing and very good accompaniment mean need only trouble himself to hear our Kapellmeister Bach here who plays every continuo to a solo in such a way that it might be thought an *obbligato* piece with the right-hand part composed previously. (L. Mizler, 1738.)

Concerning the 'third kind' of accompaniment, with intricate melodies, counterpoints, etc:

> The excellent Bach was especially capable at the third style; when he played continuo, the principal part shone out. A lifeless piece was inspirited by his very skilful accompaniment. He could bring in imitations with his right or left hand [*sic*] so cleverly, or introduce a countersubject so unexpectedly, that listeners could not believe that it had not been very carefully pre-composed. He did not nevertheless neglect his duty of supporting the harmony . . . Generally speaking, his accompaniment throughout was as a solo part worked out with industrious care and of equal importance to the principal part – which was allowed to stand out at the right moments. (J. F. Daube, 1756.)

Of directing the ensemble:

> As a young man, and until old age, he played the violin in a firm penetrating manner, by these means keeping the orchestra together better than he could have done with a harpsichord . . .

And of trio sonatas:

> Above a thinly figured continuo part set in front of him, and knowing that the composer would not object, [he converted trios] into complete quartets, astonishing the composer. (C. P. E. Bach, letter to Forkel, 1774?)

> One always had to be prepared to see Bach's hands and fingers suddenly

mingle with the hands and fingers of the keyboard-player, and, without getting in the player's way, fill out the accompaniment with masses of harmony, which overawed him even more than had the unsuspected presence of the strict master. (J.C.Kittel, 1808.)*

But the rules at the end of Anna Magdalena's book and those copied out from Niedt's *Musicalische Handleitung* (1700, copied *c.* 1738) support C.P.E.Bach's claim in his letter to Forkel that his father taught pupils strict four-part thorough-bass. One of J.S.Bach's pupils H.N.Gerber realized, or rather harmonized—it is impossible to say which—a violin sonata by Albinoni and had it corrected by his teacher; it is worked in plain four-part chords and suits the harpsichord only in that some of the chords are restruck and not tied—perhaps the ties were mistakenly omitted.

Such distinctions between Bach the skilful performer and Bach the careful teacher are easily understood; it may be a rough guide to the difference expected between a *continuo* realization on the harpsichord in theatre or chamber, and harmonic support on the organ in church. The former, composed often in imitation of Italian styles, was described by Mattheson and Heinichen, the latter by Werckmeister, Niedt and most of the German theorists. Figured bass became very much a means of learning classical four-part harmony—we have the vestiges of the method today—while the plainness of the resulting 'German style' suited the accompanying instrument most familiar to musicians in church or chamber: the organ. The realization of part of an aria in Cantata No. 3, which is given in Volume Two, page 109, is not only straightforward four-part harmony but is by its simplicity very suitable for the organ (with Stopped Diapason 8′ drawn). Moreover, such plain chords support, and do nothing to attract the ear away from, the main theme, which is in the bass. The style of this contemporary realization is consistent with that of Bach's pupil J.P.Kirnberger who gave a four-part working-out of the bass of the *Musical Offering* trio (Example 11).[15] Here, it must be admitted that the plain chords 'pull together' the *appoggiature* of the soloists, although it is true they do not make very idiomatic keyboard music: there are better, more flowing ways of accompanying *appoggiature* and avoiding doubled discords, as the player can discover for himself.

---

* Kittel's remarks concern performances of church music, when 'one of Bach's most capable pupils always had to accompany on the harpsichord' (*Flügel*). Although Kittel was himself very likely 'one of Bach's most capable pupils', this is still not reliable evidence that a harpsichord took part in cantatas at St Thomas, since (*a*) *Flügel* was by 1808 a vague term; (*b*) the term may not be Kittel's own, other parts of his treatise suggesting co-authorship; (*c*) the description may have been hearsay, Kittel being 18 when Bach died; (*d*) practices may have been changing by 1750, though this is doubtful; (*e*) *Flügel* may be a mistake for *Orgel*; (*f*) the remark may refer to rehearsals, the *director musices* being unlikely to surprise an accompanist in this way during a performance.

Example 11   J. S. Bach–Kirnberger

Example 12   J. S. Bach (BWV 1030)

Both Cantata 3 and the Kirnberger example are simpler than J. S. Bach's own
'realization' of the *obbligato* to the B minor flute sonata (Example 12).

Although 'written-out realizations' are by their nature only of limited use as
models, Examples 11 and 12 do suggest two definable styles of *continuo* extemporization. The written-out *obbligato* to the second aria of the spurious cantata *Amore
traditore* (B W V 203) is, we must assume, beyond almost any player to extemporize:

Example 13   J. S. Bach? (BWV 203)

An experienced performer would probably create something similar for such pieces as the *furioso* section in Handel's Italian cantata *Lucrezia* (*O numi eterni*). Whoever wrote *Amore traditore*, the style does suggest that the work was an essay, not perfectly successful, in the flamboyant Italian style, written by a very gifted German composer who enjoyed more complex figurations than he would have found in truer Italian works like Handel's cantata *Ah! che pur troppo è vero* and the spurious *Pastorella, vagha bella*.

For later music of the so-called Berlin and Mannheim schools, the best *continuo* style was the standard German organ texture. Plain four parts suit the simple *galant* harmony very well:[16]

Example 14   G. S. Löhlein

for continuatio see Volume Two p. 33

They also suit the piano or fortepiano as an instrument, and those pianists who play *continuo* in the opening *tutti* of concertos should copy this style for such works as Mozart's piano concertos K.37, 238, 246 (partly realized by Mozart), 271, 413–15, 449 (published in 1792 with figures), and 595 (published in 1791 without figures but with the direction *col Basso*). Other concertos are unfigured.

ENGLISH BASSO CONTINUO STYLE

Although not strictly relevant to *basso continuo*, the organ accompaniment to English consort music offers interesting, if not extreme, contrasts to that of English choral music in the first half of the seventeenth century. Especially when published the latter were usually simple, although it is true that no two contemporary organ-parts to the same anthem were identical; only the plain, unfigured bass lines of the type found in the 'Tenbury Organ Book' (*c.* 1630) need filling out by the player. The three-to-five part textures in the organ parts of average composers like Robert Ramsay are well thought out and are to be taken literally, while the flowing lines of Orlando Gibbons' three-to-four part accompaniments cannot be in any way improved, much less readily improvized. In consort music the organ often contributes an even more important part. In the big five-or-six part fantasias of John Jenkins, the organ duplicates the individual imitations and enriches the ensemble with fairly sustained chords in four and sometimes five parts; in smaller pieces of a lively nature, the organ plays in varying textures (mostly four-part in Lawes, three in Jenkins, three-to-four in Giovanni Coperario) in which *one or more* parts are new contrapuntal lines as important as those of the viols themselves. Early examples of such thematically integrated organ-parts can be found in suites by Coperario, who, like composers of verse-anthems, leaves the organist very little to add himself. Example 15 is a few bars from Jenkins' descriptive piece *The Newark Siege*; the last five bars could easily be improvized by a *continuo* player, but not the first three;[17] see overleaf.

According to Roger North,[18] and extant organ parts bear him out,

> the old masters would not allow the liberty of playing from a thro-base
> figured, as harpsichords of late have universally practised, but they
> formed the organ part express; because the holding out the sound required
> exact concord, else the consort would suffer; or perhaps the organists had
> not then the skill as since, for now they desire onely figures.

Simpson's, Locke's and Blow's little treatises are explanations of harmony rather than demonstrations of the art of accompanying, and the best players certainly had a more idiomatic keyboard style. North specifically recommended that the organist play from a score instead of a figured bass because he could then see where to 'embellish his play' and put 'somewhat more airey' into his realization.[19]

7

Example 15 Jenkins

The best accompanists on the English scene from Purcell to Pasquali appear to have been influenced by the Italians. Roger North reported two characteristics which we may regard as Italian: the use of hand-plucked, gut- and wire-strung instruments, still prevalent in the later seventeenth century, and the 'mingled harmonies' practised by keyboard players—for example, mixing tonic and dominant chords before gradually resolving them. Among the many Italian violinists and keyboard-players prominent in the more secular spheres of English music* was Francesco Geminiani, who encouraged the rich Italian accompaniment so effectively that Avison had to issue warnings about players forgetting that they were *accompanists*. Chapter Two contained examples of such accompaniments; Example 16 is a nineteenth-century realization of a Purcell song in the simple style current throughout eighteenth-century England:[20]

*Alas, the Gasparini who played in London early in the eighteenth century was not, despite Burney's reports, Francesco Gasparini, author of *L'Armonico Pratico*.

Example 16 Purcell-King

Bess cloath'd in her rags and fol-ly is come — to cure her love - - sick mel-an-cho-ly

King's note:

(i) Give the singer's notes in your chord
(ii) simple chords
(iii) accompaniment assists the melody
(iv) 'chord in imitation'
(v) 'a dispersion and display of the chord'
(vi) full chord 'giving force to the word'

(vii) light chords
(viii) chord 'gently broken'
(ix) 'the accompaniment both expressing the harmony and assisting the melody'
(x) 'the chords implied, and omitted'

M. P. King was no remarkable musician and his realization is indeed simple enough to be 'clear to every capacity', as he claimed. But the following points in Example 16 were probably characteristic of the traditional English style:

(i)   the right hand follows the melody
(ii)   the singer is at all times given his note, more or less obviously
(iii)   the chords are full only at the beginning and end of phrases
(iv)   the bass is not doubled in octaves

The 7ths in bar 4 of Example 16 and other interesting chords might be the places where an accompanist today would play full chords, 'bringing out' the discords. Modern players should not imitate the impoverished imagination of a Lampe, a Miller and a King in order to be true to past English taste, any more than they should imitate the often bad spacing of German realizations. A better model for recitatives will be found with Pasquali (Chapter Two, Example 45); for a gentle accompaniment to a simple melody, a few Italian songs with *cembalo obbligato* suggest an appropriate treatment. Something like (*a*) in Example 17 will be found to suit many an English air of characteristic sweetness;[21] (*b*) is more of a text-book realization, reliable but dull:

Example 17 (*a*) Gasparini

voice

harpsichord

Gasparini's octaves may suggest that the harpsichord-player filled in the chords a little, while the right-hand part is already 'interesting' enough in its lute-like broken chords.

EIGHTEENTH-CENTURY RECITATIVE

Players will find models of recitative accompaniment in Chapter Two. Here it is enough to distinguish between three types:

(i)   *opera seria* and chamber cantatas (Italian, French, German, English)
(ii)   *opera buffa*, especially of the late eighteenth century
(iii) German church music.

German church recitative tended more and more to be accompanied by short, detached chords from organ and string bass, however long the notes were written in the score: 22

Example 18   Türk

94

Some composers began to notate the *continuo* part correctly (C.P.E. Bach *Die Israeliten in der Wüste* 1775); but, as Türk and others said, it was usually a question of writing one way and playing another. Some of J.S. Bach's cantata and Passion recitatives should also be accompanied by short organ chords, for the composer often specifies different types of organ accompaniment for different recitatives of the same cantata; so does Handel, very occasionally, in the secular cantatas. Unlike certain modern writers I do not think that short detached chords from the organ were necessarily intended for the great cycles of Bach cantatas between 1723 and about 1735 (the Passions and most of the cantatas including the Christmas Oratorio), although it would appear that the recitatives of the St Matthew Passion were performed with detached organ chords in the later version of *c.*1736. The chief purpose of detached chords was to allow the recitative text – the narrative part of Passion and cantata – to be clear and uncovered by the sustained organ tone, even by that of the soft *Rückpositiv* Gedackt 8′ stop. Voigt (1742) thought that hands lying on organ keys would give the effect of a hurdy-gurdy. Although for much music of the early seventeenth century, such as the recitative of Peri, Monteverdi and Schütz, or the violin music of Italian and German composers, sustained organ tone brings out the contrast between its simple triadic harmonies and the quicker, lyrical line of the soloist, Protestant church cantatas of Bach's period demand different treatment. The size and acoustics of an average German hall-church, with the choir singing behind the congregation, require every possible aid if the Biblical or meditative recitative is to be clearly understood; short organ chords are certainly one of these aids.

In the case of harpsichord *continuo*, on the other hand, even the late German writers thought a richer style proper: fast and short arpeggios played by both hands with full chords, according to Hahn (1751). It is in recitatives that the French-Italian *coulés* and *acciaccature* become most useful. All theorists of note observed that recitative required special harmonies, often more dissonant, and at the same time a freer texture on the keyboard, whether for church (serious, full of *appoggiature*, rhythmically the freest of all recitative-types), for theatre (jocose,

Example 19 Gasparini

quick, imitating normal speech) or for concert-room ('as if the singer really felt the words himself', according to Tosi).[23] It is in his chapter on recitative in *L'Armonico Pratico* 1708 that Gasparini explained his arpeggios and *acciaccature* (see Example 19).

Even minor writers of Dubugrarre's rank assume that arpeggios should be used for recitative, however infrequently they might be used in other types of music. In the chamber cantata and *opera seria* of 1675–1750, the rich texture of 'the mature Italian harpsichord style' is most suitable; but warnings were frequently given that the player should not 'keep up broken figures and arpeggio, especially in grave and pathetic recitatives' (Manfredini, 1775). Whether to repeat loud chords as a help to singers, or to sustain them and let the sounds die away, or to restrike a note or two in the held chord – all depends on the sense of the words and the mood of the piece, according to St-Lambert (1707). This is very good advice.

For recitatives in *opera buffa*, including Mozart's Italian operas, 'the Italians generally play chords all in one piece'; but a quick arpeggio can be quite as rhythmically secure and at the same time is 'much more satisfying' to the ear, according to Rameau (1760). It seems, then, that Italian *continuo* style differed according to whether the piece were quick *recitativo buffo* or stately *recitativo serio*; just as German church recitative requires detached chords on the organ, so *opera buffa* recitative requires short chords on the harpsichord – and for much the same reason: both are quick, narrative sections. According to Rousseau (page 55), by at least the late 1760s Italian recitative required plain, detached chords without ornament, while the French recitative required bigger chords filled out with graceful arpeggios. Even if the chords are held, the tone is soon lost in a theatre; provided the singer keeps reasonably to pitch, the best effects are achieved when the accompanist plays *staccato* chords, varying the touch and speed of arpeggio according to the mood of the words. The interpretation in Example 20 is unrealistic, however quickly or *quasi parlando* the singer reaches the second and third chords. Strangely enough, one is today more likely to hear good and 'correct' accompaniment to Mozart's opera recitative than to Handel's – chiefly because the style is simpler and demands less invention.

Example 20   Mozart *Le Nozze di Figaro* (Act III, Sc. 1)

THE OTHER BASSO CONTINUO INSTRUMENTS

As a representative list of instruments shows (page 25), the *continuo* group changed from period to period.* For the big performances of early opera or secular orchestral music two or more keyboard instruments (perhaps including hybrids or composite instruments like the claviorgan), a string bass, and possibly several plucked string instruments were available, while by 1730 one harpsichord or organ with a cello or a bassoon (if the solo instrument were an oboe) was all that could be expected in most performances. By the end of the eighteenth century a piano, harp, or even a cello alone might support a singer or player in a public performance. Changing modes of orchestration and conducting reflect the same trends, and none of these subjects can be treated in isolation.

Examples of realizations by the 'instruments of ornamentation' are less exuberant than reports of their playing lead us to expect, but spontaneous techniques lose much in being written down [24] (Example 21, opposite).

On the other hand, the written-out parts for the 'ornamental' instruments in some English chamber music of the period are sometimes so rich, with their duplicated suspensions, full chords, passing-notes, great sweeping figures and runs, that it is hard to imagine them played *extempore* [25] (Example 22 (*b*), page 99).

In 22 (*b*) is a little of the lutenist's† *mille belles variétés et une vitesse de main incroyable* heard in Italy at that time by André Maugars, himself a notable viol-player, and of the 'invention and variety, playing now with gentle strokes and repercussions, now with generous passage-work' recommended by Agazzari in place

---

* Or even season to season, organs being prohibited in some countries during Lent, Advent and other times. Hence plucked-string continuo instruments were sometimes specified for church music—for example, F. Milleville, *Pompe Funebri . . . Responsorii delli Matutini la Sera nella Settimana Santa . . . co'l basso continuo per lò clavicembalo, tiorba ò simil' instromento* (Venetia 1624).

† The part for lyra viol, a bowed instrument, serves to remind us that, for Agazzari, the violin could also be an 'instrument of ornamentation'. It is often overlooked that all of Agazzari's ornamental instruments (lute, theorbo, harp, lirone, cittern, chitarrone, spinet, violin, pandora) also played chords in music of this period.

Example 21 (a) Kapsberger

voice / continuo / chitarrone

Se la mia vi - ta, se___ te,___ se voi se te il mio be - ne A___

___ che fu-ggir da me,___ per dar-mi pe — ne. Se — — la___ mia vi-[ta]

(b) Archilei

Dal - le più al - te___ sfe - re,___ dal-le

liuto grosso

(Two chitarroni also accompanied the voice)

più___ al - - - - - - - - - - - te sfe - re

Example 22 *(a)* R. Tailour (1615)

voices
and viols

lute

orpharion*

* a type of pandora, see glossary, p. 28

of the endless runs played by those with 'facility of hand but little learning'.26
Such passage-work, perhaps much simplified, may have been the effect Schütz
had in mind for his *Ascension Story* (1623) when he recommended the organist or
player of the *Viola* (treble or tenor viol?) to add *passaggi* under the held or re-

(b) T. Hume (1607)

treble viol

bass viol

lyra viol 1

lyra viol 2

peated notes of the singer – '*so lange der falsobordon in einen thon weret*'. They were thus ornamental lines added by the 'instruments of ornamentation' to very simple chords held by such 'instruments of foundation' as harpsichord or organ. If, however, the plucked or bowed 'instrument of ornamentation' accompanied the voice alone and not in addition to harpsichord or organ, it would need to be less brisk, less 'ornamental'. Like other written-out accompaniments of that time, though unlike the more independent lute-parts of such composers as Dowland, Example 21 would therefore make a good model for the chitarrone part of Caccini's *Nuove Musiche* (1602) when no other instrument is playing *continuo*.

It is not in clever counterpoints and counter-melodies but in chord-repercussions that lute and guitar techniques can help the modern player who wishes to obtain some picture of the overall *continuo* effect. Baron (1727) thought that the right hand should repeat chords when the bass had longer notes, strumming on the up-beats:

r.h.

l.h.

Longer notes and their chords could be restruck in time:

$\frac{4}{4}$ 𝅝 played as ♩ ♩ ♩ ♩ (Baron, Carulli) or ♩ ♩ ♩ (Matteis). Certainly the guitarist should play a full arpeggio on all important beats, though not the bass line itself if another *continuo* instrument were also playing. He can also make the harmony more interesting than it appears by introducing discords.[27]

Example 23 (a)

(b) Sanz (1674)

(c) F. Corbetta

With chords restruck, the guitar would be strong enough to accompany a single voice, though harpsichord or theorbo would no doubt be fuller for this purpose (Campion, 1716). In fuller consort or orchestral groups,

> I must allow that the attendance of instruments of the *arpeggio* kind,
> which rattle plentifully, as harpsichords, archlutes, and above all the
> pandora, give a fulness as well as elegance to the sound

wrote Roger North in the 1720s,[28] referring to practices just 'within the memory of man.' Precisely what the more brittle-toned of the plucked instruments played can be guessed. Mace gave formulae for lute-players 'to show you the way of *Amplifying* your *Play*, by *Breaking* your *Parts*' or chords (1676, pp. 221–8) (Example 24). Like Mattheson's broken-chord figures for harpsichord, such realizations are more for solo 'division' playing than for *continuo* accompanying; but the two functions of performing were probably closer in 1670 than in

Example 24   T. Mace, 1676

1720. Mace's many 'broken parts' must indicate how the better lutenists of the time interpreted their part. The two passages in Example 24 follow different conceptions of decoration, the first with full chords on the beat followed by arpeggios, the second with the bass note alone on the beat followed by a more subtle 'breaking' of the harmony – the sort of thing familiar to players of Froberger's and Louis Couperin's harpsichord music. The lower octaves of the second example agree with Agazzari's advice [29] to players to use the low bourdon strings of the theorbo or chitarrone in graceful broken chords (*passaggiando leggiadramente gli suoi bordoni*).

The sustaining bass instruments had two purposes: to play the bass line and, in the case of certain instruments, to play chords. Cellos and other bass instruments played chords in some early *continuo* groups and perhaps throughout the period whenever there were no keyboard instruments present. Agazzari recommends 'long, clear and sonorous bows' on the *lirone* or *lira da gamba* (the bass string-instrument),

> bringing out its notes as strong as the context demands, it being the foundation of good counterpoint and music-making (*caverne le parti con molto giuditio, & fondamento di buon contrapunto, & pratica*)*

The violone or great bass viol plays the bass line (*procedere fondamente*) sometimes at the octave below, 'supporting the harmony of the other instruments' (*parti*). Agazzari's phrase *toccando in dolce consonanza gli bassi & contrabassi* is important for understanding early practice, for it has several possible meanings: (*a*) 'playing the bass and its lower octaves in sweet concordance' with other instruments; (*b*) 'playing the bass with its lower octaves when the harmony is concordant', as at cadences; (*c*) 'playing the bass and its lower octave together with correct chords' on the other strings of the viol. It is unclear whether *consonanza* means 'concordance, harmony' or (as often in Italian sources) 'chords' – in which

---

* Arnold, page 72, Strunk, page 429 and Donington, page 108, translate *caverne le parti* as 'bringing out the middle parts well', as if Agazzari were referring to the cello playing chords in addition to the bass line. This appears to me, however, not to be the meaning, though the term *parti* is certainly ambiguous.

case *consonanze* might be expected. The interpretation (*c*) would mean that the violone sometimes played chords, as later did the double bass (from a figured part) for special effect in Meyerbeer's opera *Les Huguenots*. Either way, it is important that the violone could play at the octave below. This was evidently its function in the famous *continuo* group of nine instruments heard by Agazzari in an unnamed church: two harpsichords, three lutes, two chitarroni and two *violone continoi in contrabasso*.

If softly played, a trombone could replace the violone (Agazzari) and a bassoon could strengthen the bass line (Praetorius). But in a fuller consort even several bassoons could not replace a violone; they

> have more of the sound than effect of a base; for being sounded onely
> by small reeds, the force is weak, and doth not urge the other instruments,
> as the double violls doe,

in the words of Roger North.[30]

While the gamba and/or violone took the whole bass line, however quick its notes, some writers like St-Lambert and Edward Miller suggested that the harpsichord-player restrict himself to the main beats only. Runs and passing notes could be left to the string instrument – good advice for modern players who all too often keep up an endless harpsichord chatter, whether the music is soft or loud, serious Handel or light Haydn.

Also important is the evidence that *continuo* cellos and gambas sometimes played chords, especially in the later eighteenth century. J. J. F. Dotzauer, for instance, still gave advice on figured bass in his *Violoncelloschule* (*c*. 1832), and Robert Lindley applied his cello *continuo* technique to the recitatives of *Don Giovanni*. It is probably safe to assume that cellists played chords only (or chiefly) when there were no keyboard instruments. But gambas play chords naturally well, either as the sole *continuo* instrument or in addition to the others:

Example 25   J. S. Bach *St Matthew Passion* (Pt. II)

Kreuz ge-zwung-en sein;   je mehr es un-srer See-le gut,   je her-ber geht es ein.

The cello took over such functions in church and opera, according to J. F. Fröhlich in his tutor of about 1819. As did some other authors, J. Baumgartner (1774) explained chords as slurred notes or as double-stops:

Example 26   J. Baumgartner

and realized the figured bass in recitative very sparsely. Such examples support the idea that organists at that time accompanied recitatives with short, detached chords :[31]

Example 27   J. Baumgartner

*One of the three cadences in this recitative played without waiting for the singer to finish.

8

106

REFERENCES

Full titles are given in the Handlist of Books, opposite.

1. O. Kinkeldey *Orgel und Klavier* p. 153.

2. J. Haar 'Notes on the *Dialogo della Musica* of A. Doni' *ML* XLVII (1966) 219.

3. O. Kinkeldey *Orgel und Klavier* p. 167ff.

4. Bernhard/Schütz in J. Müller-Blattau *Die Kompositionslehre Heinrich Schützens* (Kassel 1963) pp. 83–4; Luzzaschi from O. Kinkeldey *Orgel und Klavier* p. 286ff; Viadana from G. Gallico 'L'Arte dei *Cento Concerti ecclesiastici* di L. Viadana' *Quaderni della Rassegna Musicale* III (1965) 55–86.

5. Ed. A. Sandberger *Monteverdi's Orfeo, Facsimile des Erstdrucks* (Augsburg 1927) p. 81.

6. A. Agazzari *Del Sonare*; also in M. Praetorius *Syntagma* III, p. 141. Praetorius' example, p. 144.

7. G. Antoniotto *L'Arte*, pl. 54; also quoted in part by A. Toni, *Sul basso*, as coming from an anonymous MS at Modena.

8. Vivaldi in W. Kolneder *Aufführungspraxis bei Vivaldi* (Leipzig 1955) p. 85, who does not mention the registration as explaining the right-hand compass.

9. See Handlist, and under L. Landshoff. Examples 7 and 8 are from the MS RI in the Biblioteca Corsiniana, Rome, ff. 43, 44, 45, 49, 49′ and (Ex. 8) 66–68′. For Scarlatti's cantatas, see E. Hanley *Alessandro Scarlatti's Cantate da Camera* (Yale Dissertation 1963).

10. J. Mattheson *Critica Musica* (Hamburg 1722) p. 195. But much more likely is that Mattheson was copying Raguenet (*Parallèle des Italiens et des Français*, 1702), who reported hearing Corelli, Pasquini and Gaetani play together. See O. Strunk *Source Readings in Music History* (New York 1950) p. 487.

11. G. F. Handel *Werke* ed. F. Chrysander, XLVIII pp. 112–17.

12. Le Cerf de la Viéville in Bourdelot *Histoire de la Musique* I (Paris 1725 edn.) p. 297.

13. *Historisch-kritische Beyträge* I (Berlin 1754) p. iv.

14. L. Mizler *Musicalische Bibliothek* I, iv (Leipzig 1738) p. 48; J. F. Daube *General-Bass* p. 204, note h; C. P. E. Bach in H. T. David & A. Mendel *The Bach Reader* (New York 1945) p. 277; J. C. Kittel *Der angehende praktische Organist* (Erfurt 1808) quoted in F. T. Arnold *Accompaniment* p. 344 (German). Another translation of the three excerpts can be found in David & Mendel, op. cit., pp. 231, 256, 266.

15. J. P. Kirnberger *Grundsätze* III (*c.* 1781) pl. 51. I have followed some of Arnold's corrections (pp. 790–2).

16. G. S. Löhlein *Clavierschule* pp. 126–7.

17. B. M. Add MS 29290, bars 26–33; dated 1646 (autograph). Score kindly lent to me by Mrs Carolyn Coxon.

18. Ed. J. Wilson *Roger North on Music* (London 1959) p. 351.

19. *Ibid.*, p. 249.

20. Arrangement of 'Mad Bess' in M. P. King *Thorough-Bass* pp. 73–4.

21. G. Rose 'A fresh Clue from Gasparini' *MT* 1475 (1966) pp. 28–9.

22. D. G. Türk *Pflichten* p. 240.

23. Tosi-Agricola, p. 150.

24. Kapsberger *Arie passeggiate* (Roma 1612) in H. Goldschmidt *Instrumentbegleitung*; Archilei, extract from *Intermedii e concerti* (Venezia 1591) in O. Kinkeldey *Orgel und Klavier* p. 306ff.

25. R. Tailour *Fifti Select Psalms of David and others* (London 1615) parts, pp. 126–9; T. Hume *Captain Humes Poeticall Musicke* (London 1607) in *Musica Britannica* IX (1955) pp. 212–13.

26. Agazzari's letter in A. Banchieri *Conclusioni*.

27. (a) Rome, Biblioteca Corsiniana MS P 15 *Regole...per...leuto* (1720) f. 33'; (b) G. Sanz *Instruccion* (1674) pl. 14 ; (c) M. Schulz *Corbetta*, where there are several misprints.

28. J. Wilson *Roger North* p. 271.

29. Letter in A. Banchieri *Conclusioni*.

30. J. Wilson *Roger North* p. 274.

31. The last two examples from A. Schering *Leipziger Kirchenmusik* pp. 106ff., 201ff. The *Méthode de Violoncelle* published by a group of cellists (Paris 1804) also illustrated chords for the cello in recitatives.

HANDLIST OF BOOKS

ADLUNG, J. *Anleitung zur musicalischen Gelahrtheit* (Erfurt 1758)
    Edition referred to : Leipzig, ²/1783, enlarged by J.A. Hiller.

AGAZZARI, A. *Del Sonare sopra il basso* (Siena 1607)
    Reprinted in Agazzari's *Sacrae Cantiones ... Liber II* (Venetiis 1609). Indispensable.

AGAZZARI, A. *Copia d'una Lettera* (1606)
    In A. Banchieri's *Conclusioni nel Suono dell'Organo, Op. XX* (Bologna 1609).

ALBERT, H. *Anderer Theil der Arien* (Königsberg 1640) preface
    Volume II of *Arien* dedicated to Schütz.

ALBRECHTSBERGER, J.G. *Principles of Accompaniment or Thorough Bass ... Translated ... by J.J. Jousse* (London [1810?])
    cf. J.G. Albrechtsberger *General-bass-schule* (Wien c. 1806) 'new enlarged edition'; and *Sämmtliche Schriften über Generalbass* 3 vols. (Wien ²/1837) ed. Ignaz, Ritter von Seyfried.

ANON [G. Carissimi?] *Kurtzer jedoch gründlicher Wegweiser* (Augsburg 1689)
    Later edns. 1692, 1693, 1696 (enlarged), 1700, 1708, 1718, 1753, 1758. Known to Mattheson (1731, p. 11).

ANON [F. von Freudenberg?] *Kurtze Anführung zum General-Bass* (Leipzig 1728)
    Later edns., 1733, 1744. Known to Mattheson (1731, p. 14) and Adlung (1783, p. 762).

ANON *Regole piu necessarie e universale per accompagniare il Basso continuo ... leuto o gravicembalo ...* 1720 (Rome, Bib. Corsiniana Mus. MS P15, ff. 28–35')

ANTONIOTTO, G. *L'Arte Armonica* 2 vols. (London 1760)
    Anonymous English translation. Copy in Rome, Bib. Sta. Cecilia with some notes by Arne.

ARNOLD, F.T. *The Art of Accompaniment from a Thorough-Bass as Practised in the 17th and 18th centuries* (London 1931).
    Indispensable.

AVISON, C. *An Essay on Musical Expression* (London 1752, ²/1753).

BACH, C.P.E. *Kurze Anweisung zum General-Bass, mit Exempeln über jedem Accord* (Brussels, Fonds Fétis 6487, MS II 4165)
    ed. I.A. Hamilton *Emmanuel Bach's Scales and Modulations extracted from Kurze Anweisung* (London 1850).

BACH, C.P.E. *Versuch über die wahre Art das Clavier zu spielen* 2 vols. (Berlin 1753/1762)
Later edns. vol. I 1759, 1780, 1787, vol. II 1797. English translation (with altered
chapter-numbers) by W.J. Mitchell (London 1949, ²/1951). Indispensable.

BACH, J.M. *Kurze und systematische Anleitung zum Generalbass* (Kassel 1780)

BACH, J.S. *Vorschriften und Grundsätze zum vierstimmigen Spielen des Generalbasses ... 1738*
In P.Spitta *Johann Sebastian Bach* II (Leipzig 1880) pp. 913–14, 942–50. Slightly
inaccurate copy, for seven out of the ten chapters, from Niedt's *Handleitung*; the
explanation of chords is fuller than that at the end of Anna Magdalena's Book.

BADURA-SKODA, P. 'Über das Generalbass-Spiel in den Klavierkonzerten Mozarts',
Mozart Jahrbuch 1957 (Salzburg 1958) 96–107.

BANCHIERI, A. *Conclusioni nel Suono dell'Organo* (Bologna 1608).
Reprinted 1609 (Agazzari's *Lettera* pp. 68–70); earlier edn. (or version) Lucca 1591;
Latin translation Siena 1608; later edns. 1626, 1627.

BANCHIERI, A. *L'Organo suonarino* (Venetiis 1605)
²/1611 including a 'Dialogo musicale ... sopra un Basso continuo'; later edns. 1622, 1638.
1622, 1638.

BARON, E.G. *Historisch-theoretisch und praktische Untersuchung des Instruments der Lauten*
(Nürnberg 1727)

BAUMGARTNER, J.B., *Instruction de Musique théorique et pratique à l'usage de Violoncello*
(The Hague 1774)

BAYLY, A. *A Practical Treatise on Singing and Playing* (London 1771)

BÉDOS DE CELLES, F. *L'Art du facteur d'orgues* 4 vols. (Paris 1766–78)

BEMETZRIEDER, A. *Leçons de clavecin et principes d'harmonie* (Paris 1771)
English translation 1778. Concerning improvisation.

BEMETZRIEDER, A., *Précis d'une nouvelle méthode pour enseigner les principes de la musique*
(London 1782)

BERGMANN, W. 'Some old and new problems of playing the basso continuo'. *PRMA*
LXXXVII (1960–1)
Helpful, but with a few misunderstandings.

BERNHARD, C. see MÜLLER-BLATTAU.

BERTEZEN, S. *Principi di Musica teorico-prattica* (Rome 1780)
Harpsichord-playing in ch. XV

BIANCIARDI, F. *Breve Regola per imparar a sonare sopra il Basso* (Siena? 1607)
Broadsheet. See R.Haas 'Das Generalbass-Flugblatt Francesco Bianciardis (1607)',
Festschrift J. Wolf (Berlin 1929).

BLOW, J. *Rules for playing of a Through Bass upon Organ & Harpsicon* (B.M. Add MS
34072, ff. 1–5).

BOLOGNA Conservatorio di Musica G.B. Martini, collection of anonymous MSS on
Figured Bass.
The most important are I50, I51, K22, L54, P120 (pp. 32–9), P132 (ff. 1–16'), P134,
P135 (ff. 45–92'), P140, and D117 ('Modo ò sia Regole per accompagnare il Basso con-
tinuo per la Viola da Gamba del C.S.').

BOYVIN, J. *Traité abrégé d'accompagnement pour l'Orgue et pour le Clavessin* appended to
Second Livre d'Orgue (Paris 1700)
Editions in Paris (²/1705?), Amsterdam (*c.* 1710, Dutch translation); known to
Mattheson (1731, p. 12).

BROSSARD, S. DE *Dictionnaire de Musique* (Paris 1703)
Later edns. 1705 and undated (Paris, Amsterdam).

BRUSCHI, A-F. *Regole per il contrapunto e per l'accompagnatura del basso continuo* (Lucca
1711)

BUELOW, G.J. 'The full-voiced style of thorough-bass realization', *Acta Musicologica* XXXV (1963) 159–71

CAMPION, F. *Traité d'accompagnement* (Paris 1716)
  Also printed in Amsterdam, 1716. Known to Adlung (1783, p. 761), probably through Walther's Lexicon. Italian translation in Florence, Bib. L. Cherubini MS B.2422 and AM 93.

CARULLI, F. *L'Harmonie appliquée à la guitarre* (Paris c. 1825)
  The 'first of its kind', a guide to extemporized accompaniment; cf. Carulli's *Solfèges avec Accompagnement*.

CERVELLI, L. 'Del Sonare sopra 'l basso con tutti li stromenti : Note sugli strumenti usati in Italia per la realizzazione del basso continuo', *Rivista Musicale Italiana* LVII (1955) 125–35

CHITI, G. *Contrapuncti, demonstratio varia* (Rome, Bib. Corsiniana, Mus. MS 9 bis/6)
  Useful ; see ROME.

CHORON, A.E. et FIOCCHI, V. *Principes d'accompagnement des écoles d'Italie extraits des meilleurs auteurs* (Paris 1804)

CLEMENT, C.F. *Essai sur l'accompagnement du clavecin* (Paris 1758)
  Later edn. 1765. More useful than *Essai sur la Basse fondamentale* (Paris 1762).

CORBETTA see SCHULZ

CORFE, J. *Thorough Bass simplified* [London c. 1808]
  At least two issues.

CORRETTE, M. *Le Maître de Clavecin pour l'accompagnement* (Paris 1753)
  Later edns. 1755 (?), 1790.

CORSINI MS see ROME

COUPERIN, F. *Règle pour l'Accompagnement*, ed. P. Brunold, *Oeuvres Complètes* I (Paris 1933) pp. 7–17

CROTCH, W. *Elements of musical Composition and Thorough Bass* (London 1812)
  Later edns., 1833 and 1856 (enlarged). More useful than *Practical Thorough Bass* (London 1826–8).

D'ANDRIEU, J.F. *Principes de l'Accompagnement du Clavecin* (Paris 1718)
  Known to Mattheson (1731 p. 11).

D'ANGLEBERT, J.H. *Principes de l'Accompagnement* contained in *Pièces de Clavecin* I (Paris 1689)
  Small but very important.

DART, T. 'Handel and the continuo', *MT* 1467 (1965) 348–50

DAUBE, J.F. *General-Bass in drey Accorden* (Leipzig 1756)
  'Written at Stuttgart, 28.12.54' (p. xxii).

DELAIRE, E.D. *Traité de l'Accompagnement pour le Théorbe et le Clavessin* (Paris 1690)
  Later edn. 1723. Praised by Rameau (1732, p. 5).

DONNINGTON, R., *The Interpretation of Early Music* (London 1963)

DRECHSLER, J. *Harmonie- und Generalbass-Lehre* (Wien c. 1828)

DUBUGRARRE, – *Méthode plus courte ... pour l'Accompagnement du Clavecin* (Paris 1754?)

EBNER, W. *Instruction zum General-Bass* translated from the Latin and appended by J.A. Herbst to his *Arte prattica et poetica* (Frankfurt 1653)
  Known to Mattheson (1731, p. 14).

EGGEBRECHT, H.H. 'Arten des Generalbasses im frühen und mittleren 17. Jahrhundert', *AfMw* XIV (1957) 61–82

FISCHER, J.P.A. *Korte en noodigste Grondregeln van den Basso continuo* (Utrecht 1731)

FLEURY, F-N. *Méthode pour apprendre facilement a toucher le théorbe sur la basse-continue* (Paris 1660)

FORTUNE, N. 'Continuo instruments in Italian monodies', *Galpin Society Journal* VI (1953) 10–13

GARNSEY, S. 'The use of hand-plucked instruments in the continuo body: Nicola Matteis', *ML* XLVII (1966) 135–40

GASPARINI Cantatas, see ROSE

GASPARINI, F. *L'Armonico Pratico al Cimbalo* (Venezia 1708)
> Later edns. Venice 1715, 1729, 1745, 1764, 1802, and Bologna 1713, 1722; translated as *The Practical Harmonist at the Harpsichord* (New Haven 1963); called *Musico Pratico al Cembalo* by Marpurg (*Beyträge*, p. 224). Indispensable.

GEMINIANI, F. *The Art of Accompaniment, or A new and well digested Method to learn to perform the Thorough Bass, Op. XI*, 2 vols. (London 1756–7)
> Later edn. of pt. I, *c.* 1790. French version, *L'Art de bien accompagner du clavecin* (Paris 1754); Italian translation in Bologna, Bib. G.B. Martini (MS). Very important.

GEMINIANI, F. *Rules for playing in a true Taste, Op. VIII* (London *c.* 1745)
> First issued 1739? Very important.

GEMINIANI, F. *A Treatise of Good Taste in the Art of Musick* (London 1749)

GOLDSCHMIDT, H. 'Die Instrument-Begleitung der italienischen Musikdramen in der ersten Hälfte des 17. Jahrhunderts', *Monatshefte für Musikgeschichte* XXVII (1895)

GOLDSCHMIDT, H. 'Das Cembalo im Orchestra der italienischen Oper der 2. Hälfte des 18. Jahrhunderts', *Liliencronfestschrift* (Leipzig 1910)

HAHN, G.J.J. *Clavierübung ... welcher eine Erklärung der Ziffern nebst praktischen Exempeln beigefügt sind* (Nürnberg 1750)

HAHN, G.J.J. *Der nach der neuen Art wohlunterrichtete Generalbass-schüler* (Augsburg 1757)
> Enlarged edn., 1768. More useful than *Der wohlunterwiesene General-bass-schüler* (Augsburg 1751).

HANDEL see MANN

HEARTZ, D. and MANN, A. 'Thomas Attwood's Theorie- und Kompositions-studien bei Mozart', *NMA* x 30, i (Supp.) (1965)
> Very useful.

HECK, J.C. *A complete System of Harmony* (London 1768)

HEERING, – *Regeln des Generalbasses von dem Herr Musice Heering* (Berlin, Deutsche Staatsbib., Mus MS theor. 348)
> Important 4-part realizations of Corelli's Op. I trio sonatas

HEINICHEN, J.D. *Der Generalbass in der Komposition* (Dresden 1728)
> Partial translation by G.B. Buelow (Berkeley 1966) *Thorough Bass Accompaniment according to Johann David Heinichen*. Indispensable.

HEINICHEN, J.D. *Neu-erfundene und gründliche Anweisung wie ein Musicliebender ... könne zu Vollkommener Erlernung des General-Basses* (Hamburg 1711)
> Very important.

HERTEL see SCHUNEMANN

HOLDER see KELLER

KELLER, G. *A Compleat Method for Attaining to Play a Thorough Bass* (London 1707)
> Later issues and edns. 1707, *c.* 1714, 1717, and contained in W. Holder *A Treatise of the Natural Grounds and Principles of Harmony* (London 1731) 2 issues.

KELLNER, D. *Treulicher Unterricht im General-Bass* (Hamburg 1732)
> Later edns. 1737, 1743, 1754, 1767, 1773, 1782, 1787, 1796; Swedish translation 1739; Dutch translation 1741. In the preface to 1737 edn. G.P. Telemann reported that the 1st edn. had sold 2000 copies in one year. Important.

KELLNER, J.C. *Grundriss des Generalbasses* (Kassel [1788])

KING, M.P. *Thorough Bass made clear to every Capacity* (London [1796])
Later edn. *c.* 1810.

KINKELDEY, O. *Orgel und Klavier in der Musik des 16. Jahrhunderts* (Leipzig 1910)
Indispensable for early continuo practices.

KIRCHNER, G. *Der Generalbass bei Heinrich Schütz* (Kassel 1960)
Supersedes similar studies by Birtner and Blume.

KIRNBERGER, J.P. *Grundsätze des Generalbasses* (Berlin 1781?)
Undated editions published in Hamburg and Munich, Vienna and Rotterdam. More
useful than *Die Kunst des reinen Satzes*, I (Berlin 1771)

KLEIN, J.J. *Versuch eines Lehrbuchs der praktischen Musik* (Gera 1783)

KNECHT, J.H. *Theoretisch-praktische Generalbass-schule* (Freiburg 1815?)
Later edn. 1830.

KOLLMANN, A.F.C. *A practical Guide to Thorough-Bass* (London 1802)
'*A Second Practical Guide*' (1807), 2nd edn.? German version, Offenbach, 1808.

LAMPE, J.F. *A Plain and Compendious Method of Teaching Thorough-Bass* (London 1737)

LANDSHOFF, L. 'Über das vielstimmige Accompagnement und andere Fragen des
Generalbass-spiels', *Sandberger-Festschrift* (München 1918)
Includes a long quotation from the Corsini MS RI.

LE CERF DE LA VIÉVILLE DE FRENEUSE *Comparaison de le musique italienne et de la
musique françoise*, 3 vols. (Bruxelles 1704-6)
Reprinted in Bourdelot's *Histoire de la Musique* (1715, later edns. 1721, 1725, 1726,
1743).

LOCKE, M. *Melothesia or Certain General Rules for Playing upon a Continued-Bass*
(London 1673)

LÖHLEIN, G.S. *Clavierschule oder kurze und gründliche Anweisung zur Melodie und Harmonie* I
(Leipzig 1765)
Later edns. 1773, 1779, 1782, 1791, 1804 (ed. A.E. Müller).

MACE, T. *Musick's Monument* (London 1676)
Pt. II, tutor for the lute.

MANFREDINI, V. *Regole Armoniche . . . e l'Accompagnamento del Basso* (Venezia 1775)

MANN, A. 'Eine Kompositionslehre von Händel', *Händel-Jahrbuch* X/XI (1964-5) 35-57
Very useful.

MAYER, J.B. *Complete Instructions for the Harp* (London *c.* 1800)
English translation of French treatise.

MARPURG, F.W. *Handbuch bey dem Generalbass*, 3 vols. (Berlin 1755-8)
Later edn., 1762 (vol. I). Probably the most useful of Marpurg's works; cf. Quantz.

MARTINI, G.B. *Regole per accompagnare* (Bologna, Bib. Martini MS I 51, 1761)
More useful than *Esemplare o sia Saggio fondamentale* (Bologna, 2 vols., 1774-5).

MATTEI, S. *Pratica d'accompagnamento sopra bassi numerati* (Bologna [1788])
Concerning improvisation. 19th cent. edns. 1875, etc; 1837 MS copy in Rome, Bib. Sta.
Cecilia.

MATTEIS, N. *The false Consonances of Music* (London 1682)
Tutor for the guitar.

MATTHESON, J. *Exemplarische Organisten-Probe* (Hamburg 1719)
2nd enlarged edn. called *Grosse General-Bass-Schule* (Hamburg 1731); English edition
1734.

MATTHESON, J. *Kleine General-Bass-Schule* (Hamburg 1735)
Both books concerned with improvisation.

112

MATTHESON, J. *Der vollkommene Capellmeister* (Hamburg 1739)

MATTHESON, J. *Das neu-eröffnete Orchester* (Hamburg 1713)

MENDEL, A. 'On the keyboard accompaniments to Bach's Leipzig church music',
MQ XXXVI (1950) 339–62
Useful, but in places disputable.

MILLER, E. *A Treatise on Thorough Bass and Composition* (Dublin n.d.)
Earlier version of *Elements of Thorough Bass and Composition* (London 1787), later issue
1800.

MOZART see HEARTZ

MOZART, W.A. [?] *Kurzgefasste Generalbasse-schule* (Wien 1818)
Later edns. *c.* 1820, 1822, 1854 (London/New York). Not useful; W.Mozart the
younger?

MUFFAT, G. *An Essay on Thorough Bass*, ed. H.Federhofer (Rome 1961)
Edition of *Regulae con centum partiturae* (1699).

MÜLLER-BLATTAU, J.M. *Die Kompositionslehre Heinrich Schützens in der Fassung seines
Schülers Christoph Bernhard* (Leipzig 1926)

NEEMANN, H. 'Die Laute als Generalbassinstrument', *Zeitschrift für Hausmusik* IV (1935)

NEEMANN, H. 'Laute und Theorbe als Generalbassinstrumente im 17. und 18.
Jahrhundert', *ZfMw* XVI (1934)

NIEDT, F.E. *Musicalische Handleitung* I (Hamburg 1700)
Important and influential.

NIEDT-MATTHESON, i.e. NIEDT, F.E., *Handleitung zur Variation* (Hamburg 1706)
²/1721 'improved with comments and an appendix of more than 60 organ
specifications' by J.Mattheson.

NORTH see WILSON

OBERDÖRFFER, F. 'Generalbass', *Die Musik in Geschichte und Gegenwart* IV (Kassel 1955).
Good survey.

OBERDÖRFFER, F. *Der Generalbass in der Instrument-Musik des ausgehenden 18.
Jahrhundert* (Kassel/Basel 1939)

OBERDÖRFFER, F. 'Über die Generalbassbegleitung zu Kammermusikenwerken Bachs
und des Spätbarocks', *Musikforschung* X (1957) 61–74
Disappointing.

PASQUALI, N. *Thorough-Bass made Easy, or Practical Rules for Finding and Applying its
various Chords* (Edinburgh 1757)
Later edns. London *c.* 1765, *c.* 1770, *c.* 1790; French translation 1760; Dutch translation
1760. Very important.

PASQUINI, B. *Regole per ben suonare il Cembalo o Organo* (Münster Coll. Santini, MS,
destroyed)
Part copied in *Regole del Sig.B.P.* (Bologna, Bib. G.B. Martini MS D138(ii)).

PASQUINI, B. [Duets for two figured-bass players, B.M. Add MS 31501, interspersed
between f3′–f77′]

PENNA, L. *Li Primi Albori Musicali per li Principianti della Musica Figurata* (Bologna
1672)
Later edns. 1674, 1679, 1684, 1696; 1678 (bk. II alone).

PERRINE, – *Table pour apprendre à toucher le luth sur . . . la basse continue* (Paris *c.* 1680)

PETRI, J.S. *Anleitung zur praktischen Musik* (Lauban 1767)
Enlarged edn., Leipzig 1782.

PRAETORIUS, M. *Syntagma Musicum* III (Wolfenbüttel 1619)
Quotes Agazzari, Strozzi and Viadana. Other directions in *Musae Sioniae* VIII, IX

(1610), *Polyhymnia Caduceatrix* (1613), *Polyhymnia Exercitatrix* (1620), *Puercinia* (1621). Indispensable.

PRELLEUR, P. *Rules for attaining to play a Thorough Bass* appended to *The Harpsichord illustrated and improv'd* (London 1730)
Another issue 1731.

PRINTZ, W.C. *Des Satyrischen Componisten* II (Dresden/Leipzig 1677)
Later edn. 1696. Known to Mattheson (1731, p. 14).

QUANTZ, J.J. *Versuch einer Anweisung die Flöte traversiere zu spielen* (Berlin 1752)
Later edns. 1780, 1789; French translation, Berlin 1752; Dutch translation, Amsterdam, 1754; Italian translation, Bologna Civico Musea, 18th cent. MS; English translation by E. R. Reilly (London 1966). Accompaniment discussed in ch. 17 (vi). Ch. 17 (iv) quoted in F.W. Marpurg *Clavierstücke* (Berlin 1763). Very important.

RAMEAU, J-P. *Traité de l'Harmonie réduite à ses principes naturelles* (Paris 1722)
Accompaniment in bk. IV (known to Adlung, 1783, p. 768). English translation, 1737, 1752, *c.* 1795 (bk. IV); Italian translation in Bologna, Bib. G.B. Martini (MS).

RAMEAU, J-P. *Code de Musique pratique* (Paris 1760)

RAMEAU, J-P. *Dissertation sur les différentes méthodes d'accompagnement pour le clavecin, ou pour l'orgue* (Paris 1732)
Supersedes other, smaller accounts (1730).

REINHARD, L. *Kurzer und deutlicher Unterricht von dem Generalbass* (Augsburg 1744)
Later edns. 1750, 1761.

ROME Biblioteca Corsiniana, collection of MSS on Figured Bass.
The most important is MS RI, 'Regole per Accompagnare sopra la Parte ... d'Autore incerto', *c.* 1710. Some of the examples are also found in Mus MS 9 bis/6; see Chiti. Indispensable.

ROSE, G. 'A fresh clue from Gasparini', *MT* 1475 (1966) 28–9

ROUSSEAU, J.-J. 'Accompagnement' and 'Recitatif–accompagné, mesuré', *Encyclopédie méthodique* (Paris, from 1782) vols. XIII and XIV

SABBATINI, G. *Regola facile e bene per sonare sopra il Basso continuo nell'Organo, Manacordo, o altro Simile Stromento* (Venetia 1628)
Later edns. 1644, Rome 1669.

SAINT-LAMBERT, M. de. *Nouveau Traité de l'Accompagnement du Clavecin, de l'Orgue* (Paris 1707)
Part II of *Principes du clavecin* (Paris 1702). Contemporary edn. Amsterdam 1725?. Known to Mattheson (1731, p. 12). Indispensable.

SAMBER, J.B. *Manuductio ad organum* 2 vols. (Salzburg 1704–7)

SANZ, G. *Instruccion de musica sobre la Guitarra española* (Zaragoça 1674)
8th edn. or issue 1697.

SCARLATTI, A. *Regole per Principianti* (B.M. Add MS 14244)
Musical examples, ff. 46'–52.

SCHERING, A. *J.S. Bachs Leipziger Kirchenmusik* (Leipzig 1936)
Later edn. 1954. Important.

SCHNEIDER, M. *Die Anfänge des Basso Continuo und seiner Bezifferung* (Leipzig 1918)
Important published version of a dissertation *Untersuchungen zur Entstehungsgeschichte des Basso Continuo* (Berlin 1917).

SCHNEIDER, M. 'Die Begleitung des Secco-Recitatives um 1750' *Gluck-Jahrbuch* III (Leipzig 1917)

SCHNEIDER, M. 'Der Generalbass J.S. Bachs', *Peters Jahrbuch* 1914/15, 27–42.
Neither this nor the previous essay has been superseded.

114

Schröter, c.g. *Deutliche Anweisung zum Generalbass* (Halberstadt 1772)
   Preface dated 1754.

Schulz, m. 'Francesco Corbetta und das Generalbass-spielen', *Musikforschung* iv (1951) 371–2
   Concerning the guitar (1670).

Schünemann, g. 'Matthaeus Hertel's theoretische Schriften', *AfMw* iv (1922) 336
   Hertel's *Kurze Anweisung wie man ... Bassum Continuum vorstellen ... kann* (1669)
Schütz see Kirchner

Simpson, c. *A Compendium of Practical Music* (London 1667)
   Later edns. 1678, 1706, 1714, 1722, 1727, 1732, and later.

Sørenson, s. and others, 'Der Generalbass um 1600', *Bericht über den neunten internationalen Kongress Salzburg 1964* (Kassel 1966) p. 201

Sorge g.a. *Vorgemach der musicalischen Composition oder ... Anweisung zum Generalbass*, 3 vols. (Lobenstein 1745–7)

Speer, d. *Unterricht der musicalischen Kunst* (Ulm 1687)
   Enlarged edition 1697.

Staden, j. *Kurzer und einfältiger Bericht für diejenigen, so im Basso ad Organum unerfahren* appended to *Bassus ad Organum* part of *Kirchenmusic* (Nürnberg 1626)
   J.S.'s *Manuduction für die so im Generalbass unerfahren* (1656) known to Mattheson (1731, p. 14); same work, later edn.?

Stephan, r. 'Über das Ende der Generalbass-praxis', *Bach-Jahrbuch* xli (1954) 80–8

Strunk, o. *Source Readings in Musical History from Classical Antiquity to the Romantic Era* (London 1952)

Telemann, g.m. *Unterricht im Generalbass-spielen auf der Orgel* (Hamburg 1773)

Telemann, g.p. *Singe-, Spiel- und Generalbass-Übungen* (Hamburg 1733–5)
   Realized examples; more useful than the directions in *Musikalische Lob Gottes in der Gemeinde des Herrn* (Nürnberg 1744).

Tomeoni, p. *Regole pratiche per accompagnare il Basso continuo* (Firenze 1795)

Toni, a. 'Sul basso continuo e l'interpretazione della musica antica', *Rivista Musicale Italiana* xxvi (1919) 229
   Important; unnamed sources include Antoniotto, Manfredini and the Torelli realizations at Modena, Biblioteca Estense.

Torres j. de Martinez Bravo *Reglas generales de Accompañar, en Organo, Clavicordio y Harpa* (Madrid 1702)
   Enlarged edn. 1736.

Tosi, p.f. *Opinioni dei Cantori antichi e moderni* (Bologna 1723)
   Translated by J.F. Agricola *Anleitung zur Singkunst* (Berlin 1757).

Türk, d.g. *Kurze Anweisung zum Generalbass-spielen* (Leipzig/Halle 1791)
   Later edns. 1800 (enlarged), 1816, 1824, 1841 (enlarged); Vienna 1822. Useful.

Türk, d.g. *Von den wichtigsten Pflichten eines Organisten* (Halle 1787)
   Later edn. 1838.

Ulrich, e. *Studien zur deutschen Generalbass-Praxis in der ersten Hälfte des 18. Jahrhunderts* (Kassel 1932)
   Published version of dissertation, Münster 1931. Useful bibliography.

Valle, p. della *Della Musica dell'età nostra* (c. 1640), in *Trattati di Musica di G.B. Doni*, ed. A.F. Gori, ii (Firenze 1763)

Viadana, l. da *Cento Concerti eccliastici* i (Venetia 1602) preface
   Later edn. Frankfurt 1613, with Latin and German translations of Viadana's preface. Indispensable.

VIÉVILLE see LE CERF

VOIGT, C. *Gesprach von der Musik* (Erfurt 1742)

WERCKMEISTER, A. *Die nothwendigsten Anmerckungen und Regeln wie der Bassus Continuus, oder Generalbass wol könne tractiret werden* (Aschersleben 1698)
Later edn. 1715. Useful.

WESTPHAL, W. *Theoretisch-praktische Leitfaden zur Erlernung des Generalbasses* (Hannover [1812])

WESTRUP J. 'The Continuo in the St Matthew Passion', *Bach-Gedenkschrift* (Zürich 1950)

WIEDEBURG, M.J.F. *Der sich selbst informierende Clavierspieler* 3 vols. (Halle 1765–75)
Part II (1767) useful.

WILSON, J. *Roger North on Music* (London 1959)
Includes 'Captain Prencourt's' teaching. Very important.

ABBREVIATIONS

AfMw	*Archiv für Musikwissenschaft*
ML	*Music and Letters*
MQ	*Musical Quarterly*
MT	*Musical Times*
NMA	*Neue Mozart Ausgabe*
PRMA	*Proceedings of the Royal Musical Association*
ZfMw	*Zeitschrift für Musikwissenschaft*

INDEX OF AUTHORS AND COMPOSERS

Page references to music examples are set in italic

ACKNOWLEDGEMENTS

Edinburgh University Press wishes to make acknowledgement to the publishers of the following titles from which textual and musical extracts have been taken:

Cassell and Co. Ltd, and W. W. Norton and Co. Inc., C.P.E. Bach *Versuch*.

Novello and Co. Ltd, Purcell *Complete Works*, Wilson *Roger North on Music*.

Oxford University Press, Arnold *The Art of Accompaniment from a Thorough-Bass*.

Yale School of Music, Gasparini *L'Armonico*.

Aria Quarta.

Ere   ſeluaggie, Che per môti errate   Il piè fermate   In   queſte verdi

piaggie V dit'il mio lamento ch'a ta   lor per pietà ferma   to il ven   to.

Illide   mia Mia filli de bella M'è ſi rubella   ſi ſpietat',e ria Che mi

vede morire Che mi vede mo   rire ne vuol moi éd'il mio   cordo   glio v

di   re.